THE CHICAGO "BLACK SOX" BASEBALL SCANDAL

A Headline Court Case

Michael J. Pellowski

Enslow Publishers, Inc.

40 Industrial Road	PO Box 38
Box 398	Aldershot
Berkeley Heights, NJ 07922	Hants GU12 6BP
USA	UK

http://www.enslow.com

To Coaches Pat Dolan and Stan Potonski

Library of Congress Cataloging-in-Publication Data

Pellowski, Michael J.
  The Chicago "Black Sox" baseball scandal : a headline court case /
Michael J. Pellowski.
      p. cm.—(Headline court cases)
  Summary: Examines the 1920 trial of eight Chicago White Sox
baseball players accused of conspiracy to commit an illegal act when
they allegedly took money from gangsters to lose the 1919 World Series.
  Includes bibliographical references and index.
  ISBN 0-7660-2044-4 (hardcover)
  1. Trials (Conspiracy)—Illinois—Chicago—Juvenile literature. 2. Chicago White Sox
(Baseball team)—History—Juvenile literature. 3. Baseball—Corrupt practices—United
States—History—Juvenile literature. 4. Baseball—Betting—United States—History—
Juvenile literature. [1. Trials (Conspiracy) 2. Chicago White Sox (Baseball
team)—History. 3. Baseball—History.] I. Title. II. Series.
KF224.B57 P45 2003
796.357'64'0977311—dc21
                                       2002012524

Printed in the United States of America

10 9 8 7 6 5 4 3 2 1

To Our Readers:
We have done our best to make sure that all Internet Addresses in this book were active
and appropriate when we went to press. However, the author and publisher have no control over and assume no liability for the material available on those Internet sites or on
other Web sites they may link to. Any comments or suggestions can be sent by e-mail to
comments@enslow.com or to the address on the back cover.

Illustration Credits: AP/Wide World: pp. 21, 74, 109; Chicago Historical
Society: pp. 79 (ICHi-20727), 94 (ICHi-28764); Dover Publications: p. 9; Library
of Congress: pp. 7, 17, 26, 30, 43, 48, 55, 65, 98, 101, 113; National Baseball Hall
of Fame and Museum: pp. 13, 36, 68; Photo File, Inc.: pp. 61, 85, 89.

Cover Illustration: Chicago Historical Society (ICHi-18010); altered.

Contents

chapter one

"SAY IT AIN'T SO, JOE"

CHICAGO—"Say it ain't so, Joe."

A teary-eyed young baseball fan was reported to have uttered those words to Chicago White Sox superstar "Shoeless" Joe Jackson as the ballplayer exited a courtroom in September of 1920. The charge against Joe Jackson and teammates Eddie Cicotte, Oscar Felsch, Charles Risberg, George Weaver, Arnold Gandil, Claude Williams, and Fred McMullin was conspiracy to commit an illegal act. The crime was punishable by five years' imprisonment and a fine of up to $10,000 (a lot of money in 1920).

The eight Chicago players were accused of conspiring with a group of notorious gamblers, including underworld mastermind Arnold "The Big Bankroll" Rothstein, to fix the outcome of the 1919 World Series—to lose on purpose so that gamblers would make money betting on the games.

Did the 1919 Chicago White Sox baseball team owned by Charles A.

Comiskey lose the World Series because eight Chicago players played poorly on purpose? Were those eight players paid to lose the most prestigious games in all of baseball? Did those men dubbed "The Black Sox" by an irate press sell their integrity as professional athletes for cold, hard cash put up by gamblers and gangsters?

Many years later Joe Jackson claimed the "Say it ain't so, Joe" line was a joke.[1] He said it was a phony story dreamed up by *Chicago Daily News* reporter Charley Owens. There was no young boy waiting outside of the courthouse after Jackson testified to the Cook County grand jury.

Whether some brokenhearted young fan disillusioned by possible corruption in the game he loved ever muttered that famous phrase to his baseball idol is not really important. What is important is the truth about the role gambling played in the outcome of the 1919 World Series.

Were all of the eight players charged with conspiracy in pro baseball's most shameful incident actually guilty? Did some of the eight ignore the threats of thugs and hoodlums and truly play up to their potential in the Series? Chicago third baseman George "Buck" Weaver batted .324 in the 1919 World Series, collecting eleven hits, including four doubles and one triple. Amazingly, Weaver also made only four errors, misplaying four of thirty balls hit to him at third base, where balls streak toward the fielder because he plays so close to the batter.

"Any man who bats .333 is bound to make trouble for the other team in a ball game," Buck stated in defense of his innocence. "The best team cannot win a world's

Baseball star Ty Cobb called Joe Jackson (shown above) the greatest pure hitter he had ever seen; Jackson's glove was called "the place triples go to die."

championship without getting the breaks."[2] (Weaver actually hit .324 on 11 hits on 34 at bats, but made a mistake about his average when speaking to reporters.)

Outfielder and super-slugger "Shoeless" Joe Jackson managed to best his teammate's impressive stats by posting the top batting average in the Series. A player's batting average is determined by dividing the number of at bats he has into the number of hits he collects during those at bats. For example, if a player collects 3 hits in 9 at bats, his batting average would be .333 (3/9 = .333).

"I led both teams in hitting with .375. I got the only home run of the series. . . . I handled thirty balls in the outfield and never made an error or allowed a man to take an extra base. I threw out five men at home," Joe Jackson recalled in an interview years after the scandal.[3]

Could players who posted impressive statistics like those be guilty of compromising their ability as athletes?

"Crookedness and baseball do not mix," said Charles Albert Comiskey, owner of the White Sox.[4] It was Comiskey who personally headed up the initial investigation that brought the conspiracy to light. It was Comiskey who policed his own clubhouse and blew the whistle on his own players. He willingly destroyed what some sports experts believed was the greatest sports dynasty of its time.

Even though Comiskey championed truth in uncovering facts about the fixing of the 1919 World Series, he himself may have played a key role in causing the scandal. He was notoriously cheap when it came to players' salaries. Most of the White Sox players were underpaid. They felt they were being cheated by a stingy team owner. The best team in baseball was known to be the worst paid. That fact made bribery possible.

Professional baseball is a game of money. The team owners are in business to make money. The athletes play for money. Money was a key factor in the case against the Black Sox eight.[5]

Assistant State Attorney Hartley Replogle was in charge of the case against the accused Chicago ballplayers. "This is

Charles Comiskey, owner of the Chicago White Sox, was known as "Commy" and "the old Roman." While he was a great figure in baseball, he was tightfisted when it came to paying his players.

just the beginning," Replogle told reporters on September 29, 1920. "We will have more indictments within a few days and before we get through we will have purged organized baseball of everything that is crooked and dishonest."[6]

Hartley Replogle wanted to punish those guilty of corrupting America's national sports pastime. He wanted to restore the public's faith in the honesty of pro baseball. The tarnished reputation of pro baseball needed to be repaired quickly if the sport was to regain its fan support.

Ultimately, that task did not fall on the shoulders of Hartley Replogle. It became the job of the first commissioner of baseball, appointed by the team owners in 1920: Judge Kenesaw Mountain Landis. Landis, a federal judge, retained his position on the federal bench while also serving as baseball's top decision maker. Judge Landis was named after Kennesaw Mountain (minus an n) in Georgia where his father had been wounded during the Civil War.[7]

The commissioner's first task was to clean up the 1919 World Series scandal. The way he handled the incident is controversial to this day. Some say his judgment was harsh and unfair. Others claim he saved the sport of baseball. The question remains: Is illegal gambling still a shadowy part of professional sports? Please, say it ain't so.

chapter two

IT'S A MONEY GAME

SPORTS DYNASTY— The Chicago White Sox team has a long and rich history. The team was formed in 1900 as an original franchise of the American League. Charles A. Comiskey, a player for the old St. Louis Browns in the 1800s, assumed the ownership of the club that was originally known as the Chicago White Stockings.

In 1901 the American League became a new major league and a rival of the National League, which had been established in 1876.

Charles Comiskey's White Stockings won the very first American League title.[1]

In 1902 the White Stockings shortened their name to the White Sox. The following year, the American and National leagues agreed to meet in a season-ending championship, thus giving birth to baseball's famous World Series.

Chicago Rules

The 1906 World Series matched the American League (AL) champion Chicago White Sox against their same-city rivals, the National League (NL) champion Chicago Cubs. With solid pitching and defense, the White Sox captured their initial World Series championship.

The White Sox continually drew huge crowds of fans to their games, and in 1910 Charles Comiskey built a new home field for his club on Chicago's South Side. The ballpark was named Comiskey Park, after the owner.

In the following years, Comiskey dedicated himself to procuring the services of the best available players money could buy. Comiskey obtained his desired athletes by purchasing their contracts from rival teams. He spared no expense in getting who he wanted. However, once he owned those players' contracts, Charles Comiskey abandoned his free-spending habits. He was far from generous when it came to rewarding players for their on-field performances. It was Comiskey's custom to underpay even his key contributors. Compared to the salaries paid to other pro baseball players in the league, Comiskey's world champion White Sox were embarrassingly shortchanged.

Comiskey was able to get away with paying low salaries because of a standard reserve clause in players' contracts at the time. The controversial reserve clause bound a player to his team. The contract stated that a player signing for one year also agreed to play for the same club the year after, if the club wanted him to. Since players always signed contracts each year before being permitted to play, the reserve clause was, in effect, a contract for life. If a player turned down his team's salary offer, he could not play for anyone else. It was a take-it-or-leave-it proposition. It was

The Chicago White Sox, originally known as the White Stockings, were a powerhouse throughout the early 1900s. The team of 1919 (shown above) was widely favored to defeat the Cincinnati Reds in the World Series.

not until 1976 that signed players could become free agents (and able to sign with another team) after playing out the renewal year in their current contracts.[2]

In baseball during the 1900s there was no such thing as free agency. Players could not change teams without the permission of the team owner. A pro baseball player, even one of superstar status, had to play for the salary the team offered him or sit out the entire season.

Harry Grabiner, the White Sox club secretary who handled contracts, had a standard response for any player who grumbled about paltry pay. Grabiner would coldly state, "Take it or leave it!"[3]

Buying Victory

In 1915 Charles Comiskey purchased the contracts of three star athletes. One of those athletes was outfielder Oscar "Happy" Felsch, whom Comiskey obtained from Milwaukee. It cost Comiskey $12,000 to buy Felsch's contract. Another addition was outfielder "Shoeless" Joe Jackson from the Cleveland Indians. It cost $65,000 to obtain Jackson's rights. Lastly, the White Sox owner bought the contract of second baseman Eddie Collins from the Philadelphia Athletics. Collins's contract also cost Comiskey $65,000.[4] Of the three new additions, Eddie Collins proved to be the wisest and most farsighted. Collins was a graduate of Columbia University. He was smart enough to have his old $14,500 salary written into his new contract. Thus, Charles Comiskey was forced to pay the star second baseman a wage comparable to that of other top players of the day.[5]

Around that time Babe Ruth was a pitcher-outfielder for the Boston Red Sox and earned an annual salary of $10,000 per year.[6]

Another Championship and No Reward

In 1917 the rebuilt Chicago White Sox team topped the American League, besting such teams as the Detroit Tigers led by Ty Cobb, the Cleveland Indians with Tris Speaker, and the Boston Red Sox aided by the talents of a young, hard-throwing pitcher named Babe Ruth.

The White Sox proved to be a championship-caliber club by combining good hitting and fielding with solid pitching. Ace pitcher Eddie Cicotte won 28 games that season. Cicotte's efforts were supported by the timely hitting of Jackson, Felsch, and Collins. Veteran first baseman Arnold "Chick" Gandil played tough defense. The sure-handed play of rookie shortstop Charles "Swede" Risberg allowed veteran infielder George "Buck" Weaver to play third base, where he excelled.

The White Sox proved too strong an opponent for the NL champion New York Giants in the 1917 World Series, even though the Giants were managed by baseball legend John McGraw, who was famous for his winning ways. The Sox beat the Giants 4 games to 2 games to win the Series. Team owner Charles Comiskey had promised his players a big bonus if his team won the Series. Comiskey did not keep his word. The only bonus the Chicago players ever received was a cheap case of champagne.[7] They received no extra pay.

The White Sox players were disappointed and angered by the treatment they received from the team owner after their 1917 World Series win, but they were not totally surprised by Comiskey's cheapness. At a time when teams usually gave their players a minimum of four dollars a day for meal money, Comiskey gave his players only three dollars a day for meals. Instead of providing free cleaning for the team's uniforms like other owners did, Comiskey charged his players a laundry fee to wash their uniforms.[8] In protest, the team once refused to pay the fee and wore their uniforms until they were filthy. An angry Charles Comiskey collected the uniforms from the players' lockers, cleaned them, and promptly fined his players to cover the cost of the service.

Discord and Dissension

The 1918 Chicago White Sox seemed like a close-knit unit, but it was not a team in any sense of the word. In reality, the White Sox were split into two different cliques. The members of each clique openly disliked the other.

One group was led by slick-fielding, hard-hitting college graduate Eddie Collins. The New York–bred Collins had attended Columbia and was proud of his Ivy League education. He used his education to hold his own in bitter contract negotiations with the sly Charles A. Comiskey. Collins earned almost twice as much money as any other player on the White Sox.

Eddie Collins's closest friends on the club included catcher Ray Schalk, a Chicago native; veteran pitcher Urban "Red" Faber, who was from Iowa; and young rookie pitcher Dickie Kerr of St. Louis, Missouri. Collins's pals were a quiet and reserved group. They had vastly different tastes and interests than fun-loving party-goers Chick Gandil and Swede Risberg, both of whom were from remote areas of California.

Chick Gandil was the leader of the other clique. Risberg was his constant companion. Joe Jackson, a South Carolina farm boy, was also part of Gandil's party group. Jackson, who had trouble reading and writing, originally signed his name with an X. He later learned how to write his name. Though he was uneducated, Jackson had a good head on his shoulders and was not dumb. He just did not fit in with big-city types like Collins and Schalk. Claude "Lefty" Williams was also intelligent and enjoyed the company of fellow

Eddie Collins, shown here on a baseball card from his days with the Philadelphia Athletics, was a college-educated player who negotiated a good contract for himself.

southerner Joe Jackson. The last member of the group was Oscar "Happy" Felsch. Felsch was a native of Milwaukee, Wisconsin. He was a likeable guy who enjoyed a good time.

The other team regulars—Buck Weaver (third base), Shano Collins (outfield), Nemo Leibold (outfield), Eddie Cicotte (pitcher), and utility player Fred McMullin, who substituted at several positions—were caught somewhere between the two opposing groups. Weaver and McMullin usually went along with Gandil, while Shano Collins (no relation to Eddie) and Leibold were part of the Collins crowd. Pitcher Eddie Cicotte was a loner.

The resentment between the two groups was so intense that Gandil and Risberg refused to speak to Eddie Collins. By the 1919 World Series, the three teammates had not exchanged a friendly word in nearly two years. During infield warm-ups, first baseman Chick Gandil and shortstop Swede Risberg would not even throw a ball to second baseman Eddie Collins. Chick and Swede knew they were underpaid and hated Eddie because he was not.

Gandil and Risberg also disliked catcher Ray Schalk. They did not care for his candid off-field attitude or his on-field hustling style of play. They always excluded Ray Schalk from their conversations. Schalk was not bothered by the fact that two of his teammates would not speak to him. Ray Schalk disliked Gandil and Risberg as much as they disliked him.[9]

The Chicago White Sox were talented, but they were also a team in turmoil. Nevertheless, under the leadership of manager William "Kid" Gleason, the Sox battled the

Cleveland Indians down to the wire for the championship of the American League in 1919.

Broken Promises

Before the 1919 baseball season began, Comiskey told his star pitcher Eddie Cicotte that if he won thirty games that year, he would receive a $10,000 bonus.[10] With strong support from his teammates, Cicotte recorded 29 victories on the pitching mound as the season progressed. He needed only one more win to collect his bonus as the season neared its end. To prevent Cicotte from earning victory number thirty and the bonus, Comiskey ordered team manager Kid Gleason to bench his number one pitcher. Reluctantly, Gleason obeyed. Cicotte was never given the opportunity to win game number thirty or to cash in on the promised bonus. Comiskey denied that Cicotte was benched to keep him from collecting the extra money. The White Sox owner claimed that he was giving Cicotte a rest so he would be fresh for the World Series at the end of the season. The truth of the matter will never be known. However, Cicotte and his Chicago teammates did not believe Comiskey's story. In fact, the situation infuriated Eddie Cicotte. He openly swore to get even with his tightwad team owner and voiced his displeasure with Comiskey's handling of players. One player who paid close attention to Cicotte's frequent complaints was first baseman Chick Gandil.

Gandil and friends were also fed up with Charles Comiskey's penny-pinching ways and his broken promises.

Unlike modern athletes who have the bargaining power of a strong players' union, pro baseball players of the time had no one to turn to for help in dealing with team owners or league officials.

The White Sox players were stifled at every turn in their dealings with Comiskey. They could not even turn to the press for help or support. Rather than spend money on players, Charles Comiskey wined and dined members of the press so they would portray him in a favorable light. A special room at Comiskey Park was reserved for members of the press. It was always filled with expensive food and drinks, which were served free to all media representatives. It was no wonder many reporters believed Comiskey to be a friendly and generous man.

Another League Championship

The Chicago White Sox, guided by Kid Gleason, managed to win the 1919 American League crown by edging the Cleveland Indians in the final standings. The White Sox posted a season record of 88 wins and 52 losses to capture first place, while the Indians finished second, with a record of 84 wins and 55 losses.

In the National League, the Cincinnati Reds, managed by Pat Moran, surprised baseball experts by catching and then surpassing the league-leading New York Giants in late August. The Reds won their very first NL title by posting a final record of 99 wins and 44 losses. The Giants tallied 87 wins and 53 losses to capture second place in the standings.

Catcher Ray Schalk (right) was disliked by the members of Chick Gandil's clique because of his candor and his energetic playing style. He is shown here with William "Kid" Gleason, former manager of the White Sox, in a 1927 photo.

When the skills and personnel of the two league champions were compared, the White Sox seemed superior in almost every way. The American League champions were a star-studded team. The National League champion Reds were looked on as a group of hardworking but ordinary athletes. Cincinnati was led by sluggers Ed Roush, Jake Daubert, and Alfred Earle "Greasy" Neal. Their pitchers—Hod Eller, Jimmy Ring, and Dutch Reuther—were good, but not great. On paper, Chicago held an advantage over Cincinnati in almost every category.[11]

Experts like sports reporters and other students of the game, including some coaches, declared that the Chicago White Sox were the favorites to win the Series. Unofficially, bookmakers, or "bookies" (those who accepted wagers and paid the winners) gave odds in favor of the Sox. This meant they believed that the Sox were so much better than the Reds that it was highly unlikely that Cincinnati could win. To tempt bettors to wager on the less-favored team, bookmakers offered to pay out two, three, or more dollars for every dollar bet. For instance, odds of 3 to 1 mean that there would be a payout of three dollars for every dollar bet. The odds given against the Reds winning the World Series were 5 to 1. No one seriously believed Cincinnati had a chance to win baseball's coveted crown.

Baseball and Gambling

After the American Civil War, public interest in baseball soared. In the sport's early days, baseball—like horse racing and boxing—attracted the interest of professional gamblers.

At the time, betting on the outcome of an athletic contest seemed innocent enough. Friendly wagers on games played between neighboring towns or rival groups were part of the fun. However, as interest in games grew, the wagers became less friendly.

Years later, when baseball became a professional sport, there were attempts to eliminate betting on the outcome of pro contests. In 1876 the National League was formed. At that time, regulations were adopted that restricted the sale of alcoholic beverages at ballparks and prohibited players from betting on their own games. The league penalty for betting on games by a player was banishment from baseball for life.[12]

Despite the harsh punishment for betting on games, professional baseball had several hushed-up incidents of gambling prior to the 1919 World Series scandal. As early as 1876, players were accused of "fixing" the outcome of baseball games by playing badly on purpose. The Louisville Club, run by Charles Chase, was involved in a scandal when several members of the squad were involved in a bribery scheme. Players Al Nichols, George Hall, and Jim Devlin received about one hundred dollars each to play badly in a series of games against a weaker club from Hartford, Connecticut. When Louisville lost to Hartford, Charles Chase confronted Nichols, Hall, and Devlin. The players admitted their guilt. Their case was taken before league president William Hulbert. He promptly banished the players involved in the scheme from pro baseball for life.[13] Hulbert absolutely refused to consider the players' excuse that they had accepted the bribes only because their own team had never paid their salaries.

Another incident of illegal betting in baseball occurred in 1917. A hard-hitting first baseman named Hal Chase (no relation to Charles Chase) played for the Cincinnati Reds in 1917. Chase was a gifted athlete. He also had a dark side to his personality. Hal Chase liked to associate with gangsters and gamblers. Chase's teammates and friends suspected him of betting on the outcome of his own games. In 1917 Chase tried to bribe one of his teammates to do badly in a game and ultimately lose the contest.

When pitcher Jimmy Ring was brought in to help win a game, Hal Chase went to the mound. "I've got money bet on this game, kid," Chase is reported to have told the young pitcher. "There's something in it for you if we lose."[14]

Ring did not win the game, but he did not lose on purpose. Nevertheless, Hal Chase later slipped Jimmy Ring a fifty-dollar bill. Ring took the money to his manager, Christy Mathewson, and told him what Chase had said. Mathewson reported the incident to league president John Heydler, who conducted a hearing. Hal Chase was acquitted because John Heydler did not feel there was enough evidence against him.

Christy Mathewson made his own decision about Chase. He traded the first baseman to manager John McGraw's New York Giants. Throughout his career, baseball officials suspected Chase of playing his best only when it suited him.

League president John Heydler had him watched closely by umpires to see if he played badly on purpose. In 1919

Heydler advised the Giants staff that Hal Chase and teammate Heinie Zimmerman were suspected of being involved in baseball betting schemes. Once again, there was not enough evidence to make a case against the players. However, time was running out for Hal Chase as an athlete. The year 1919 turned out to be his last year as a pro baseball player. Chase remained involved in sports betting circles for many years after his playing days ended.[15]

Gandil Gets the Ball Rolling

Arnold "Chick" Gandil knew Hal Chase. The two men were similar in many ways on and off the field. Gandil and Chase were both athletic first basemen. They were both friendly with gangsters and gamblers. Most of all, both men were not afraid to bend rules to make easy money.

In 1919 Chick Gandil was thirty-one years old and rapidly approaching the end of his playing career. Although he was a member of a world championship team, Gandil was making only $4,000 a year. Other big-league first basemen were making much more. For example, first baseman Jake Daubert of the Cincinnati Reds was earning $9,000 a season.

Gandil was an aging athlete with little hope of living a comfortable life after his sports career ended.

"By the time of the 1919 Series, you could say I had been around," Gandil once told reporters. "Although past my peak, I still hit .290 and had the best first-base fielding record in the league."[16]

Chick Gandil decided he needed to make some big money fast if he wanted to retire in comfort. Past experience

Chick Gandil, a first baseman, was past his athletic peak at the time of the 1919 World Series. A friend of gangsters and gamblers, he was looking for a way to make some easy money for his retirement.

had taught him that there would be no bonus if the Sox won the World Series as expected. It was Gandil who hatched the plot of fixing the outcome of the 1919 World Series. He knew gamblers who could assist him in his scheme. He also had influence over other disgruntled Chicago players. All the ingredients for the fix were at his disposal.

Gandil's decision to fix the game was not a snap judgment. He knew he could not throw the Series without help. Weeks before the Series began, Chick Gandil began to lay the groundwork for that assistance. He hinted to star pitcher Eddie Cicotte that some people could make a lot of money if the Series ended with the right results. At the time, Gandil was testing Cicotte to learn if he could be corrupted. Gandil had no concrete plans. He needed money before he could make any deals.[17]

chapter three

A SLIDE INTO THE DIRT

THE FIX—Star pitcher Eddie Cicotte of the Chicago White Sox had a reputation for being a family man who enjoyed the simple life. Cicotte was a good husband and a devoted father of two young children. In 1919 he and his wife purchased a farm in Michigan. There was a large mortgage on the farm.[1] Cicotte was worried about paying that mortgage. He did not make enough money as a baseball player to be financially secure.

Cicotte was not a man who normally associated with gamblers or gangsters. He had no history of betting on baseball games to make extra money. All he wanted was to make a good living playing professional baseball. He wanted what he felt was due him as a professional athlete and a key player on a championship team.

At the time of the 1919 World Series, Eddie Cicotte was thirty-five years old. He realized his best years as a pitcher were probably already behind him. His arm was starting to lose its strength and vigor. He was now using all the tricks he could think of to gain an advantage over batters.

Teammate Chick Gandil compared White Sox Pitcher Cicotte to pitcher Walter Johnson, who played for Washington, winning 802 games during his long career and ending up in pro baseball's Hall of Fame. "Only Walter Johnson was better," said Chick Gandil of Cicotte. "He knew all the tricks."[2]

Shoeless Joe Jackson agreed with Gandil. "Cicotte was the best pitcher in the league next to Walter Johnson," Jackson once said.[3]

Nevertheless, in 1919 pitcher Eddie Cicotte was earning less than $6,000 a year as the ace pitcher of the Chicago White Sox. Once before, team owner Charles Comiskey had found a sneaky way to keep from paying Cicotte a well-deserved bonus. Cicotte's dislike for Comiskey had grown intense and was well known to the Chicago players. The fact that Eddie was in need of cash to meet his financial obligations was also well known to his teammates.

At first Eddie Cicotte refused to listen to Chick Gandil's World Series proposal. He wanted no part of any wrongdoing. Gandil kept after Cicotte. He presented the scheme as a way to make easy money and a way to get back at Comiskey. After a while, the plan began to sound a bit more attractive to the angry and desperate Cicotte. The lure of big money became more and more difficult to resist.[4]

The Ballplayers

Arnold "Chick" Gandil's plan to fix the 1919 World Series had no hope of succeeding unless star pitcher Eddie Cicotte

Eddie Cicotte was one of the best pitchers of his era; however, he was underpaid compared with star players on other teams.

was a part of the conspiracy. The services of other Chicago ballplayers would also have to be bought if the plan was to work. In addition to Gandil and Cicotte, six others were picked to play badly in exchange for bribe money paid to them in advance by gamblers. The conspirators were a group of pitchers, infielders, and outfielders.

Claude Williams—Pitcher. Twenty-six-year-old Claude "Lefty" Williams was the other star pitcher of the Chicago White Sox. Williams won seventeen games in 1917 when the White Sox captured the World Series. He improved his mound record to twenty-three pitching victories in 1919. Even though his statistics were excellent, Williams earned less than $3,000 a year as a White Sox player.

Chick Gandil assessed Williams's pitching ability: "Basically better than Cicotte, he won games the conventional way, good curve and fastball, excellent control."[5]

Charles Risberg—Shortstop. Charles "Swede" Risberg was the youngest member of the conspirators. The twenty-five-year-old infielder was a rising star with a bright future. Nevertheless, he was paid less than $3,000 a year for his services as a professional athlete. Risberg was a rough and tough player who never backed away from fights on or off the field. Joe Jackson described Risberg in simple, no-nonsense terms. "Swede is a hard guy," Joe Jackson said of the young Chicago shortstop.[6]

Fred McMullin—Infielder. Fred McMullin was a twenty-seven-year-old utility player—one who is the backup player for several different positions. McMullin was a key reserve who batted .294 in 1919. He knew the game of baseball and also knew he would never achieve star status as a player. McMullin earned less than $3,000 in 1919. He was very interested in Gandil's plan to make extra money.

Oscar Felsch—Center Field. Oscar "Happy" Felsch came to the White Sox in 1915. Charles Comiskey bought out Felsch's contract for $12,000. In 1919 Felsch was a twenty-eight-year-old who earned only $4,000 a year. Happy Felsch was a swift defensive outfielder who hit .275 in 1919. He also hit 7 home runs that year to share the team lead in that category with Joe Jackson. One thing that did not make Felsch happy was the salary he was paid by the White Sox.

George Weaver—Third Base. George "Buck" Weaver could hit and field with the best of baseball's top players of the time. When the White Sox captured the American League pennant in 1919, Buck was twenty-nine years old and still had an excellent future in baseball. Weaver hit .296 in 1919, collecting 169 hits, which was second only to Joe Jackson's team-leading total of 181 hits. Nevertheless, Weaver earned only $6,000 a year. Players on the White Sox team knew Buck was vastly underpaid as a professional athlete.

Joe Jackson—Left Field. Shoeless Joe Jackson was a player destined for Baseball's Hall of Fame. He was a solid defensive player and one of the game's greatest hitters. He could do it all on a baseball diamond.

"I consider Joe Jackson the greatest natural ballplayer I've ever seen," said pitcher Walter Johnson.[7]

Jackson got his famous nickname as a young outfielder playing minor-league baseball in Greenville, South Carolina. He played for Greenville before moving up to the major leagues to star with the Philadelphia Athletics.

Joe Jackson was a poor South Carolina farm boy at the time. He had a new pair of spiked baseball shoes that he did not feel comfortable wearing. The shoes gave young Jackson blisters and hurt his feet. Joe took off the shoes during a game and played several innings of the contest in his stocking feet. After Jackson made a good play, an opposing fan stood up to jeer at Joe. The fan shouted, "You shoeless son of a gun you!"[8] Soon everyone was calling

Jackson "Shoeless Joe." The nickname stayed with him throughout his career.

Shoeless Joe Jackson saw limited action with the Philadelphia Athletics in 1908 and 1909. He hit .387 as a reserve for the Cleveland Indians in 1910. In 1911 Jackson hit an astonishing .408 for Cleveland as a starter for the Indians. From that year on, Joe Jackson posted exceptional batting averages in the high 300s. He quickly established himself as one of the game's best hitters.

Charles Comiskey purchased Shoeless Joe Jackson's contract from the Cleveland Indians in 1915 for $65,000. Four years later, thirty-year-old Joe Jackson was earning just $6,000 as a star outfielder for the Chicago White Sox.

In 1919 Jackson led the Sox with 181 hits, including 7 home runs. He also had 96 RBIs (runs batted in). Joe posted an impressive .351 batting average that season. Chicago second baseman Eddie Collins batted .319 that year and had only 165 hits, 4 home runs, and 80 RBIs. Collins's totals were far less than Jackson's totals. Yet Collins was paid more than twice as much as Jackson. Comparing the productivity of the two players shows just how unfair owner Comiskey's salaries were.

The Fix

The interest of gamblers in major-league baseball games was a real concern to baseball officials in 1919. The game of baseball is not sports entertainment like modern professional wrestling is. The outcome of baseball contests is not supposed to be predetermined. Baseball officials were afraid that gamblers might try to fix the outcomes by bribing players secretly. Charles Comiskey was so worried about the influence gambling might have on game results that he posted signs in his stadium reading "NO BETTING ALLOWED IN THIS PARK."[9]

White Sox player Chick Gandil paid no attention to Comiskey's signs. He had already gotten shortstop Swede Risberg to agree to help him throw the 1919 World Series. Now Risberg and Gandil were pestering pitcher Eddie Cicotte to join forces with them. For the time being, Cicotte still refused to participate in the crooked scheme.

One day, Chick Gandil and Swede Risberg were discussing their secret World Series plans in the Chicago locker room. Utility infielder Fred McMullin overheard the two conspirators. He heard Gandil promise Risberg that they would make a "financial killing" on the World Series if they could pull off their plan.[10]

McMullin was not part of the original group Gandil planned to recruit, because he was not a starting player. Fred McMullin forced Chick Gandil to include him. McMullin wanted to be cut in on the easy money Gandil said could be made.

However, the key piece to the big fix puzzle was still pitcher Eddie Cicotte. The conspirators needed Cicotte's cooperation to make the plan work. Chick Gandil, as the ringleader of the group, also needed money to pay off his coconspirators before the World Series began. Gandil planned to enlist the aid of several well-known gamblers of the time. He would get the bribe money from them. The gamblers' reward would be knowing in advance which team would win the 1919 World Series. They could place bets with no risk of losing.

The Gamblers

Chick Gandil knew several types of gamblers. Some were gangsters who wagered large sums of money on various sporting events. Others were crooked ballplayers.

Hal Chase. In 1919 Hal Chase was a first baseman for the New York Giants. Chase had also played for the New York Yankees and the Washington Nationals. He had been involved with betting on baseball games before, but had never been caught at it. When the White Sox played the Yankees in New York late in the 1919 season, Gandil and Chase had bumped into each other. Rumors were already buzzing around pro baseball locker rooms about a possible World Series fix. Hal Chase had heard them. He wanted to place a few bets of his own so Chase asked Gandil if there was any truth to the rumors. Gandil did not confirm or deny the rumors.

Joseph Sullivan. Joseph "Sport" Sullivan was a big-time gangster and bookmaker. Joseph Sullivan knew Chick Gandil before Gandil played for the White Sox. Chick used to give Sport inside tips on games when Gandil played for the Washington Nationals baseball team.

William Burns. William "Sleepy" Burns was an ex-ballplayer who had spent several years as a pitcher in the major leagues with various teams. He had a career record of 29 wins and 55 losses. Burns got his nickname because he

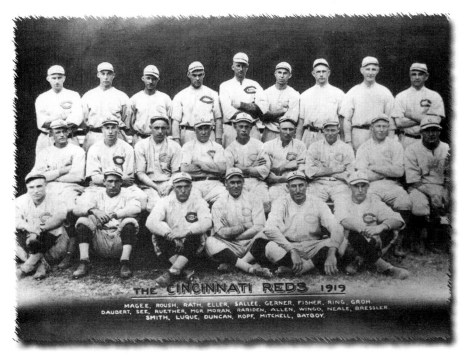

THE CINCINNATI REDS 1919

MAGEE, ROUSH, RATH, ELLER, SALLEE, GERNER, FISHER, RING, GROH.
DAUBERT, SEE, RUETHER, MGR. MORAN, RARIDEN, ALLEN, WINGO, NEALE, BRESSLER.
SMITH, LUQUE, DUNCAN, KOPF, MITCHELL, BATBOY.

The Cincinnati Reds, National League champions, were hardworking ballplayers, but they were widely considered to be the underdogs in the 1919 World Series against the White Sox.

had been known to fall asleep on the bench during ball games.[11] Bill Burns was a casual friend of Eddie Cicotte. After retiring from baseball, Burns worked in the oil industry in Texas. He was also friendly with big-time gamblers around the country.

Bill Maharg. Bill "Billy" Maharg was an ex-boxer and a semipro baseball player. He made a lot of claims about his playing past, but had little or no evidence to support those claims. Maharg had been a member of the big-league

Detroit Tigers for one day in a strange but historic game against the Philadelphia Athletics. On May 19, 1912, the regular Detroit Tiger players refused to play and called a strike because their star player, Ty Cobb, was suspended and unable to participate in the contest. To make sure the game was played as scheduled, the Detroit officials signed semi-pro players for just that one game. Bill Maharg was one of the players they recruited. He turned to gambling as an occupation after his athletic career ended.

There is some question about Bill Maharg's true baseball background. Maharg is the name Graham spelled backward, and Billy had an uncanny resemblance to a former major-league catcher named Peaches Graham. Some believe Graham and Maharg were one and the same.[12] However, it remains one of baseball's unsolved mysteries.

Abe Attell. Abe Attell's real name was Albert Knoehr. Knoehr changed his name to Attell when he turned to pro boxing to make a living. Abe was also known as "The Little Champ."[13] Attell got the nickname because he weighed only about 116 pounds yet had a spectacular record in the ring: He won 365 professional fights and lost only 6 bouts. Some of those six losses were questionable. Attell was suspected of losing on purpose to help gamblers win their wagers. After a very suspicious loss in 1912, Abe Attell was suspended from professional boxing.

One of the gamblers Abe Attell was friends with was Arnold Rothstein. The Little Champ met Rothstein in 1905. The two had a working relationship that bordered on friendship. Attell ran errands and did odd jobs for Rothstein.

He also acted as a bodyguard for the big-time gambler. Rothstein enjoyed the companionship of the ex-fighter. The two men went many places together.

Arnold Rothstein. "Arnold Rothstein is a man who waits in doorways . . . a mouse, waiting in the doorway for his cheese," said attorney William J. Fallon, describing his famous client.[14] Rothstein was so well known that his vast influence as a gambler was referred to in F. Scott Fitzgerald's classic American novel *The Great Gatsby.*

Arnold "The Big Bankroll" Rothstein was a native New Yorker who enjoyed the company of athletes and sportsmen. Rothstein was often referred to as a sportsman himself. In reality, he was just a well-bred professional gambler. He got the nickname "The Big Bankroll" from his habit of always carrying a fat roll of crisp hundred-dollar bills. Rothstein made money because he was capable of financing any attractive proposition on the spot. Arnold Rothstein claimed he was always willing to bet on anything except the weather. The weather was excluded from his gambling interest because it was too unpredictable and could not be fixed. Arnold Rothstein liked to bet on sure things.

Money Talks

Big-time gamblers like Arnold Rothstein and Abe Attell were willing to pay out large sums of money if the outcome of the 1919 World Series could be arranged in advance. Chick Gandil's persistence finally paid off with Eddie Cicotte. The promise of a big payday that would ensure the financial security of his family convinced Cicotte to be party to the fix.

"I was thinking of the wife and kids and how I needed the money," Cicotte explained after the true story of the scandal broke a year later. "I told them I had to have the cash in advance. I didn't want any checks. . . . I wanted the money in bills. I wanted it before I pitched a ball."[15]

Eddie Cicotte's price to throw the World Series was $10,000. With Cicotte on the payroll, Gandil was finally ready to move forward with his plan to arrange the outcome of the 1919 World Series.

Enter Sport Sullivan

Chick Gandil now needed cash to buy the cooperation of his teammates. On a road trip to the East Coast in September 1919, Chick Gandil contacted an old gambling pal—Joe "Sport" Sullivan. The two men arranged to meet in Boston to discuss the 1919 World Series fix. Gandil told Sullivan that the 1919 World Series could be bought. The total price was $80,000. The money would be paid out in bribes to the Chicago players, including Gandil. Sport Sullivan was very interested in the deal, but he did not have that kind of money to pay out. He told Gandil he knew someone who did have that kind of cash: Arnold Rothstein. Sullivan promised to arrange everything, and the men parted company.

A short time later, the White Sox traveled to New York City to play the Yankees. During the trip, Gandil realized he needed the cooperation of another pitcher on his team to make sure the fix would work. He decided to recruit Claude "Lefty" Williams. While in New York City, Chick Gandil told Lefty Williams about the plan.

Throw the World Series? At first, Claude Williams was sickened by the thought of such a thing. He refused to believe it was possible. Gandil assured Lefty that a conspiracy did exist and that the fix would be pulled off with or without his help. When Williams still hesitated, Chick Gandil told Lefty Williams that Eddie Cicotte was already a party to the conspiracy. Hearing that his fellow star pitcher was in on the fix disturbed Williams. He promised to think over Chick Gandil's proposal. Gandil believed Williams would eventually agree to be part of the scheme. He was correct.

Three More Make Eight

Chick Gandil had lined up Chicago's two top pitchers. He also had shortstop Swede Risberg and utility man Fred McMullin on his side. He feared the Series could not be lost with those five players alone. He decided to recruit Chicago's best hitters in the batting order to his cause. Those three batters were George "Buck" Weaver, "Shoeless" Joe Jackson, and Oscar "Happy" Felsch. The three men were also members of Gandil's usual circle of friends.

Chick Gandil arranged to have Weaver, Jackson, Felsch, and Williams meet with him, Risberg, McMullin, and Cicotte. The eight men met in Gandil's hotel room on September 21, 1919.

"Gandil was the master of ceremonies," Cicotte told reporters a year later. "We talked about throwing the Series. Decided we could get away with it. We agreed to do it."[16] Gandil told his teammates about the $80,000 they would divide up between them if they lost to Cincinnati.

Buck Weaver listened to the proposal but was noncommittal. He did not agree or disagree. Happy Felsch joked about stupid ways errors could be made to ensure a victory for the Reds. Shoeless Joe Jackson did not say anything. Gandil took their behavior to mean consent. In his mind the fix was officially on. However, to the others it was just talk. No money had changed hands. In fact, Weaver and Jackson did not actually agree to accept a bribe if it was offered to them.

Meanwhile, gambler Bill Burns was in New York City on business at the same time. By pure chance, he bumped into his old friend, Eddie Cicotte. Sleepy Bill had heard the rumors about a possible World Series fix. Rumors had been circulating since Chick Gandil met Sport Sullivan in Boston. Burns asked his friend Cicotte if there was any truth to them. Cicotte reluctantly confirmed Sleepy Bill's suspicions. The Series could be bought. The players were now waiting to see some actual cash.

Small-time gambler Bill Burns saw an opportunity to become a big-time player in the gambling world. He begged Cicotte not to accept money from anyone until the two men could meet again. Burns planned to get the bribe money himself.

Bill Burns quickly got in touch with a local gambling associate named Billy Maharg. Maharg operated out of Philadelphia, Pennsylvania. Billy Maharg went to New York City to meet with Bill Burns. The men met in the same hotel where the White Sox players were staying. Burns and Maharg met with Chick Gandil and Eddie Cicotte. Gandil told the two gamblers the price of fixing the outcome of the World Series was now $100,000. The gamblers agreed to pay that sum because they could make much more betting on fixed games.

The Money Man

The truth was that Billy Maharg had no hope of raising $100,000. He did not have the resources himself, but he did know where to go to get some cash quickly. A scheme the magnitude of a World Series fix would surely interest Arnold Rothstein. Rothstein could easily come up with $100,000.

Days later Bill Maharg and Bill Burns approached Arnold Rothstein at a local racetrack. With Rothstein was Abe "The Little Champ" Attell. Rothstein politely told the two small-time gamblers he did not have time to listen to their proposal and calmly walked away. Minutes later, he had a change of heart and sent Attell back to hear the men out.

Maharg and Burns explained that they could fix the outcome of the 1919 World Series if Rothstein would put up $100,000 in bribe money. Attell later repeated the plan to Rothstein in private. Arnold Rothstein did not believe Burns

Third baseman Buck Weaver met with the gamblers and the crooked players, but never agreed to fixing the Series.

and Maharg could arrange such a big fix. He refused to give them the cash.

Bill Burns and Billy Maharg were devastated by Rothstein's refusal. Next, Burns sought out the assistance of another former player and associate, Hal Chase. Burns met with Chase in a New York City pool hall. It was a place frequented by New York Giants baseball players.

The two men discussed the fix. Chase advised Burns to go back and meet with Arnold Rothstein again. He told Burns where to find Rothstein. When Burns asked him what he wanted in exchange for his help, Hal Chase declined any reward. He told Burns the opportunity to bet on a rigged Series would be reward enough. Chase later informed Rube Benton, a teammate of his on the Giants, about the fix.[17]

Burns and Maharg went off to sell their scheme to Arnold Rothstein. The two men were waiting when Arnold Rothstein entered the lobby of the Ansonia, a famous New York hotel. Once again, they approached the wealthy gambler with their proposal. Once again, "The Big Bankroll" refused to get involved with them or their scheme. Rothstein did not believe two small-time gamblers like Burns and Maharg could arrange the biggest fix in sports history.

Billy Maharg finally gave up and went back to Philadelphia. Sleepy Bill Burns also forgot about fixing the World Series and turned his attention to his oil business. Abe Attell, however, was sold on the Gandil scheme even if his boss was not. He believed the World Series could be fixed.

Abe Attell went to the New York hotel where Bill Burns was staying. He told Burns that Rothstein had changed his mind and would come up with the cash. The story was a total lie. Attell was bluffing in the hopes of making money on the betting scheme himself. Bill Burns believed Attell and was convinced that Rothstein had the bribe money ready to pay out.

The Big Bankroll Pays Up

After Arnold Rothstein refused to bankroll Bill Burns and Billy Maharg's scheme, Joe "Sport" Sullivan showed up at his door with the very same proposition. This time, Arnold Rothstein listened attentively. Rothstein knew of Sullivan's reputation as a big-time gambler. He believed someone like Sullivan really could fix the World Series. Rothstein sent Nat Evans, one of his trusted henchmen, to check up on Sullivan's claim. Evans, using the phony name of Brown, went to Chicago along with Sullivan to meet with the eight White Sox conspirators. Brown and Sullivan met with Chick Gandil on September 29, 1919, the day before the World Series was to begin in Cincinnati. Brown was quickly convinced that the players were in earnest and would follow through on their promise to throw the Series.

However, Chick Gandil now had doubts about his own plan. Some of his coconspirators were starting to balk. Lefty Williams wanted out of the shady deal. Joe Jackson was being evasive. Lefty claimed to speak for Joe, who was now said to want $20,000 for his part in the scheme. Buck Weaver was not saying or doing anything. Eddie Cicotte, on the other hand, delivered an ultimatum to Chick Gandil and Swede Risberg.

"The day before I went to Cincinnati I put it up to them squarely for the last time," Cicotte later revealed, "that there would be nothing doing unless I had the money."[18]

Cicotte's demands had to be dealt with immediately. He was scheduled to pitch the first game of the 1919 World Series. Brown promised Gandil that the players would be paid off by Sullivan. The fix was definitely a done deal.

True to his word, Arnold Rothstein sent $40,000 to Sport Sullivan in Chicago. The money was to be paid to the players before the World Series began. Another $40,000 was sent and placed in the safe of the Hotel Congress in Chicago. It was to be paid to the players after the Series was over and Cincinnati had won the 1919 World Series.

Double-Crossed

As soon as he was convinced the 1919 World Series was rigged, Arnold Rothstein began to place bets on the underdog Cincinnati Reds. Some reports claim Rothstein bet over $250,000 on the Reds to win at the Series.[19]

Hal Chase also made large bets on the Reds to win, although the amounts he wagered were far less than Rothstein's bets.

On a tip from Sport Sullivan, even the famous dancer, actor, and playwright George M. Cohan wagered money on the underdog Cincinnati Reds to win the 1919 World Series.[20]

Sport Sullivan, who was given $40,000 of Arnold Rothstein's money to pay the players, also made some bets. He also secretly stole $10,000 of the $40,000 and wagered it on the Cincinnati Reds. The many bets being placed on the Reds made Cincinnati less of an underdog in gambling circles. It appeared that many people actually believed the Reds stood a good chance of winning the Series, so the odds offered by bookmakers began to fall.

Sullivan took $10,000 of the remaining $30,000 and gave it to Chick Gandil. He told Gandil more money would be available soon. Gandil was angry about the amount but accepted the payoff. He had no choice. The White Sox conspirators had already worked out which games they would purposely lose to throw the Series. They needed to be bribed to carry out the plan. The problem was that $10,000 would not go very far when divided among the conspirators.

All of the "Black Sox Eight" were supposed to be paid before the Series began. There was only enough money to satisfy the demands of Chicago's starting pitcher for Game One of the World Series. That pitcher was Eddie Cicotte.

"That night I found the money under my pillow," said Cicotte. "There was $10,000, I counted it. I don't know who put it there but it was there. It was my price."[21] Eddie Cicotte sewed his bribe money into the lining of his jacket. He was now on the take and paid to lose.

Chick Gandil was no longer concerned about Eddie Cicotte. Cicotte had been paid. He also knew he could rely on Swede Risberg and Fred McMullin to make sure things would turn out the right way in the Series.

From the early days of baseball in the late 1800s, fans thronged to ballparks in eager support of "America's game." Shown is the crowd at the 1910 unofficial World Series between the New York Nationals and the New York Americans.

However, Chick Gandil was not sure of Lefty Williams. Williams seemed to be wavering. Chick Gandil also did not have a clue where Buck Weaver stood in regard to the fix. Weaver had sat in on every meeting the players had about throwing the World Series, but he never spoke for or against the scheme.

The player of biggest concern was Shoeless Joe Jackson. Initially Gandil had offered Joe $10,000 for his part in throwing the Series. Jackson had snubbed the offer. Lefty Williams, Jackson's close friend on the team, still claimed to speak for Joe and said his price was $20,000. The amount was an ongoing quarrel between the conspirators. When Gandil made the offer of $10,000 to Jackson personally, Joe flatly refused it.

Gandil then supposedly told Jackson to take it or leave it because the fix was already on and the White Sox would lose the Series with or without his assistance.[22] Gandil did not know if Jackson was in or out.

According to Jackson in an interview years later, he was definitely out. When he was approached with the initial offer of a $10,000 bribe, Joe refused to participate. Hugh Fullerton, a reporter from the *Chicago Herald and Examiner,* is said to have witnessed Shoeless Joe's refusal to accept cash in return for playing poorly.[23]

Jackson later claimed he was worried about his involvement with the conspirators. He did go to team manager Kid Gleason and owner Charles Comiskey and begged to be kept out of the lineup against Cincinnati. He did not tell them his reasons for the odd request. Gleason and Comiskey ignored Jackson's plea not to be part of the 1919 Series. Shoeless Joe was expected to play and he would play. It did not matter that Gleason and Comiskey were starting to hear rumors regarding a possible fix of the 1919 World Series.

Gamblers Hard at Work

Abe Attell followed up on his deal with Sleepy Bill Burns and went to Cincinnati to raise the $100,000 needed to pay off the White Sox players. Attell did not know that Rothstein had already funded the deal through Sport

Sullivan. Arnold Rothstein did not know that Attell was still involved in any way.

The Little Champ contacted every gambler he knew and collected enough cash to place some bets for himself on Cincinnati. Bill Burns and Billy Maharg traveled to Cincinnati and went to the hotel where the White Sox team and Attell were staying.

When Burns and Maharg met with Attell, they found Abe's room full of new associates. They were gamblers Attell had already borrowed money from. Abe had used the money to make bets and had no cash to give Burns and Maharg for the Chicago players. Attell tried to calm Bill Burns. He assured Burns that everything would turn out well. Abe himself would meet with the players and explain what was going on.

That meeting was held in Chick Gandil's room at the hotel. Seven members of the Chicago White Sox were present. Shoeless Joe Jackson did not attend the meeting. Abe Attell told the seven players he had the money to pay them, but the payoff was to be staggered. The players would receive $20,000 after each loss in the Series. When the Reds finally captured the 1919 Series with five wins, the total payoff to the White Sox players would equal the agreed-upon $100,000. (The 1919 World Series was a best of nine games series rather than a best of seven game series, which it is today. The owners thought playing a longer series would attract more paying fans and more money would be made.) The payments for losing the game would be delivered to the players by Sleepy Bill Burns after each loss.

Once again, the players were angry but agreed to the terms. They would play and wait to be paid afterward.

The only player who was not disappointed was pitcher Eddie Cicotte. Unlike the others, he had already been paid off and was ready and willing to throw Game One of the Series.

chapter four

THE SCANDAL THAT ROCKED BASEBALL

SERIES BEGINS—The opening game of the World Series between the Cincinnati Reds and the Chicago White Sox was held at Cincinnati's Redland Field on October 1, 1919. The stands were full of excited fans eagerly awaiting the umpire's cry, "Play ball!"

The noisy throng of baseball buffs quieted for the playing of the national anthem. John Philip Sousa, the world-famous composer, conducted the band in "The Star Spangled Banner."[1]

Finally, it was time to play. The starting lineups were posted. The lineup for the Chicago White Sox was:

1. Shano Collins— right field

2. Eddie Collins— second base

3. Buck Weaver— third base

4. Joe Jackson— left field

5. Happy Felsch— center field

6. Chick Gandil— first base

7. Swede Risberg—shortstop

8. Ray Schalk—catcher

9. Eddie Cicotte—pitcher

The lineup for the NL champion Cincinnati Reds was:

1. Morrie Rath—second base

2. Jake Daubert—first base

3. Heinie Groh—third base

4. Edd Roush—center field

5. Pat Duncan—left field

6. Larry Kopf—shortstop

7. Greasy Neale—right field

8. Ivy Wingo—catcher

9. Dutch Reuther—pitcher

Game One

Chicago pitcher Eddie Cicotte hit Cincinnati's leadoff batter, Morrie Rath, in the back with the second pitch of the ball game. The bad pitch puzzled White Sox catcher Ray Schalk, since Cicotte normally had pinpoint control. A select group watching the game was not puzzled by the unusual occurrence. Hitting Rath was a secret, prearranged signal that the 1919 World Series had been fixed. As the game wore on, Schalk's puzzlement changed to fury. Cicotte continually ignored the catcher's signals, which told him which pitches to throw. Instead of throwing the ball hard, Cicotte threw pitches that were easy to hit. The Cincinnati batters clobbered Cicotte's pitches. Jake Daubert and Greasy Neale collected three hits each.

The Cincinnati pitcher, Dutch Reuther, had no problem containing the Chicago hitters. The Sox seemed baffled by Dutch's pitches. Reuther also excelled at the plate. As a hitter, he clouted two triples and a single in three at bats. He also batted in three runs.

Eddie Cicotte did his best not to fool the Reds hitters by throwing curve balls or other trick pitches. He threw straight pitches of medium speed. There was no spin on the ball, and it was easy for the eye to track. "I wasn't putting a thing on the ball," Eddie Cicotte later confessed. "You could have read the trademark on it when I lobbed the ball up to the plate."[2]

Since Cicotte was not putting anyone out, and hitters were knocking baseballs around almost at will, manager Kid Gleason decided to take Cicotte out of the game in the fourth inning. Cicotte was replaced by relief pitcher Roy Wilkinson with the score 6–1 in favor of the Reds. Cincinnati ended up winning the game 9–1.

Pitcher Eddie Cicotte was not the only player who helped his team lose. Swede Risberg and Chick Gandil played key parts in the Chicago defeat. During the game, Gandil was tagged out at second base, ending a scoring opportunity for Chicago. Risberg misplayed a ball that would have resulted in a double play (when two runners are put out on a

Eddie Cicotte hit Morrie Rath (shown at right), the leadoff batter for Cincinnati, with the second pitch in the first World Series game. This signaled to the gamblers that the game was fixed.

single batted ball). Shortstop Risberg also dropped a pop fly ball he could have caught. The mishaps helped the Reds win Game One.

After the opening-day loss in the 1919 World Series, Chicago manager Kid Gleason and catcher Ray Schalk suspected all was not right with their team. They were both boiling mad after the disappointing upset. Back at the team's hotel, Gleason screamed at Cicotte and Gandil in the hotel lobby. The White Sox manager was so mad he had to be pulled away from Cicotte and Gandil by reporter Hugh Fullerton. If Fullerton had not stepped in, there may have been a fight between Gleason and his players.

Other people were not as upset as Kid Gleason. Gambler Bill Burns could not have been happier about the outcome of Game One. Burns had bet money on the Reds to win. He had already cashed in on the fix one time and planned to do it again. Burns met up with Billy Maharg. Together they went to Abe Attell's room to collect payoff money for the players. Once again, Attell claimed he had no bribe money

purpose. Gleason planned to voice his opinion to team owner Charles Comiskey.

When Comiskey heard what Gleason had to say, he did not believe it. Nevertheless, Comiskey went to see National League President John Heydler to discuss the possibility that the games had been fixed. Heydler was one of three members of pro baseball's governing body, the National Commission. The other two members of the commission were August Herrmann and Byron Banfield "Ban" Johnson. Comiskey did not consult directly with Herrmann, because he was the owner of the Cincinnati Reds. He did not talk with Ban Johnson, the president of the American League, because Johnson and Comiskey had been enemies for many years.

In fact, when John Heydler did tell Ban Johnson about Comiskey's concerns regarding fixed games, Johnson dismissed Comiskey's worries, claiming they were "the yelp of a beaten cur."[3] No one on the National Commission believed the World Series could be fixed. They did not believe Comiskey or Gleason. They thought it was impossible to fix the World Series. They were wrong.

After the second Chicago loss, Bill Burns and Bill Maharg went to see Abe Attell. Burns and Maharg demanded money to pay off the Chicago players. Attell did not want to pay. He begrudgingly came up with the sum of $10,000, which Burns delivered to Chick Gandil. Gandil took the money, but he was angry. He had expected the sum of $40,000, which the gamblers and conspirators had already agreed on.

Game Three

The third game of the 1919 World Series proved to be a real shock to the gamblers involved in the fix. They believed the White Sox players were their powerless pawns. They learned otherwise. Pitching for Chicago in the third game of the Series was Dickie Kerr. Kerr was a small lefthander. Famous writer Damon Runyon penned these words about Richard Kerr:

> Take Dickie Kerr, now, a wee hop o' my thumb. Not much taller than a walking stick . . . the tiniest of the baseball brood. Won't weigh 90 lbs soaking wet, an astute scout once reported after a look at Kerr . . . a left-handed pitcher. Too small for too much of anything, except, perhaps, a watch charm.[4]

Dick Kerr was a small man, but he had a big heart when it came to pride in his athletic ability. He could not be intimidated. Although many of his own players were working against him, Kerr pitched a tremendous game against the Reds. The gamblers were expecting the White Sox to lose. The plan was for Chicago to lose the first three games of the Series and then win the fourth game so as not to arouse too much suspicion. The gamblers were double-crossed by the White Sox conspirators with help from Dickie Kerr.

It took Kerr less than ninety minutes to dispose of the Reds. Cincinnati managed only three hits and lost the game, 3–0.

Pitcher Ray Fisher was the losing pitcher for the Reds. The hitting stars for the Chicago White Sox were Joe

Jackson and Chick Gandil. Gandil singled and drove in two of Chicago's three runs. Swede Risberg and Happy Felsch also contributed to the win. The Chicago players on the take turned the tables on the gamblers. Instead of losing as they were supposed to, the conspirators played hard and helped Dickie Kerr win the game. The gamblers lost money because they had the wrong information and had bet on Cincinnati. It became obvious that the gamblers would have to pay for the cooperation of the White Sox conspirators. The players would no longer throw games unless they were paid in advance.

Gamblers Abe Attell and Sport Sullivan had not paid Chick Gandil, Swede Risberg, and their coconspirators the money promised to the players. Therefore, the players doublecrossed the gamblers. Sportswriters covering the Series and some baseball experts were becoming suspicious. How could the White Sox play so well one day and so badly on other days? Trouble was brewing on all sides. Gamblers Attell, Burns, and Maharg had lost a lot of money on Game Three and no longer trusted the players. The players did not trust the gamblers. Only Arnold Rothstein was unconcerned. He had not bet on individual games. He had wagered on the Reds to win the 1919 World Series.

Abe Attell refused to give the players any more money. Sport Sullivan tried to resolve the players' problems. He hurriedly raised $20,000 in cash. He promptly delivered it to Gandil to distribute among the players before Game Four. Lefty Williams, Happy Felsch, and Swede Risberg received $5,000 each. Williams reportedly placed $5,000 cash in an

Dickie Kerr's excellent pitching upset the plans of those betting on Game Three. Rather than losing as arranged, the Sox won, 3–0.

envelope and took it to Joe Jackson's room. Buck Weaver received no money. Neither did Fred McMullin. (Chick Gandil already had the $10,000 Bill Burns had given him earlier.)

Game Four

Eddie Cicotte was back on the mound for Chicago in Game Four. Pitching for the opposition was Jimmy Ring. Sportswriters and fans alike expected Cicotte to redeem himself for his opening-day loss. For a while it seemed as if Cicotte would do just that.

The game remained scoreless until the fifth inning. Reds left fielder Pat Duncan grounded back to pitcher Eddie Cicotte with one out. Much to everyone's surprise, Cicotte misplayed the ball and then threw it over Chick Gandil's head at first. The error allowed Duncan, who should have been out, to advance to second base. Duncan ended up in scoring position.

Cicotte then promptly gave up a single to Larry Kopf. The ball fell into left field in front of Joe Jackson. Duncan tried to score. Jackson picked up the ball and made a perfect throw to home plate. It looked like Duncan would be out at home for certain. Suddenly pitcher Eddie Cicotte rushed over. The ball bounced off Cicotte's glove for an error—Cicotte's second error in the inning. Instead of being out at home, Duncan scored easily. The next Reds batter was Greasy Neale, who belted a Cicotte pitch over Joe Jackson's head for a double. Larry Kopf scored on the hit. The Cincinnati Reds won Game Four, 2–0. The

Reds now needed only two more victories to claim the World Series crown.

Game Five

Lefty Williams pitched for Chicago in Game Five. He was matched against Hod Eller of Cincinnati. Williams pitched well, holding the Reds hitless for four innings. Hod Eller pitched even better. After giving up two harmless hits in the first, he struck out Chick Gandil, Swede Risberg, and Ray Schalk in the second inning. In the following inning, he struck out three more Chicago batters. The next inning, Eller fielded two soft ground balls and threw out both runners at first. He then struck out the next White Sox hitter. The Cincinnati pitcher himself accounted for nine straight outs.

In the sixth inning, the Reds batters began to hit Chicago's Lefty Williams. They received some help from Happy Felsch, the Chicago center fielder. Felsch misplayed one fly ball and dropped another. His errors allowed four Cincinnati runners to score. The Reds scored another run in the ninth inning to win, 5–0. Lefty Williams lost his second World Series contest. Williams and Cicotte, who had combined for fifty-two Chicago wins during the regular season, were 0–4 in the World Series. It did not seem possible.

Extra Money

In 1919, participating in a World Series did not guarantee that the players would receive a lot of extra money. After the conclusion of Game Five, the attendance records of the first five games were made public. The attendance at the games was important because the ballplayers received a share of the money collected from the fan support in those five games. After Game Five, the players were excluded from any further profit sharing. The money collected after Game Five was divided only among the two club owners and the National Commission. It was not a very fair system. According to the gate receipts for the first five games, each player on the winning team of the 1919 World Series would collect an additional $5,000. The members of the losing team would be paid $3,254 each. Winning a championship did not mean players became instantly rich. It could be more profitable to be bribed to lose.

Game Six

Dickie Kerr again pitched for the White Sox as the Series returned to Cincinnati. The opposing pitcher for the Reds was Dutch Reuther. Reuther was the pitching hero for the Reds in Game One. The two men were equally matched in talent.

Chick Gandil and his fellow conspirators had not received the bribe money due them after Game Five. Since they were not paid to play poorly, they played as well as they could. Buck Weaver, Joe Jackson, and Happy Felsch hit so well that pitcher Dutch Reuther was replaced by relief pitcher Jimmy Ring. Ring did not have much better luck getting out the Chicago batters. The White Sox beat the Reds, 5–4, and Dickie Kerr recorded his second World Series victory.

Game Seven

"Cicotte is going to win today," manager Kid Gleason told sportswriter Hugh Fullerton before Game Seven of the 1919 World Series. "He came to me this morning and he told me that he wanted to pitch. He said he would beat those guys and I believe him."[5]

According to plans made with the gamblers before the Series began, Eddie Cicotte was not supposed to lose Game Seven. Cicotte pitched the way he was capable of, and his teammates played up to their potential. Eddie Cicotte dominated the Cincinnati batters, and the Sox topped the Reds, 4–1, to earn their third World Series victory. The Series was now 4 games to 3 in favor of the Reds. Gamblers began to get nervous. Arnold Rothstein in particular did not like the sudden and unexpected turn of events. The gamblers were not sure if the fix was on or off.

For Game Eight of the Series, Claude "Lefty" Williams was scheduled to pitch for

Walter "Dutch" Reuther excelled at both pitching and hitting for the Reds in the first game of the Series, but had to be relieved by Jimmy Ring in Game Six. The Reds lost, 5–4.

the White Sox. People with gambling interests in the Series wanted to make sure Williams understood the danger he was in if the game did not turn out the way it was supposed to.

A gangster known only as Harry F. went to see Lefty Williams and his wife. It is unknown who sent Harry F. to visit with the couple. It was suggested that he had been sent by Sport Sullivan. Others think that he was obeying orders from Arnold Rothstein. Harry F. warned Lefty Williams to be careful when he pitched. He told him not to last past the first inning on the mound. If Williams pitched well against the Reds, Harry F. told them, he and his wife might get hurt.

Game Eight

The Series shifted back to Chicago. Nearly 33,000 fans crammed into Comiskey Park to witness what they hoped would be a miracle comeback by the Sox. But Williams was so frightened by the threats of Harry F. that he dared not pitch well. Instead he lobbed easy-to-hit "meatballs" at the plate. The Reds took a 4–0 lead in the first inning. Lefty Williams was replaced by relief pitcher Bill James. James was later replaced by Roy Wilkinson. Hod Eller pitched the entire game for the Cincinnati Reds.

Despite the hard-hitting efforts of Buck Weaver, Joe Jackson, and Eddie Collins, the White Sox never recovered from the game's disastrous start. Chicago lost the game, 10–5, and also lost the 1919 World Series crown.

Sportswriter Hugh Fullerton had heard rumors of a fix all through the Series. He had also been witness to an attempted bribe of Chicago outfielder Joe Jackson. In several articles, Fullerton had hinted to the public that some of the White Sox players may have been paid by gamblers to play poorly. The 1919 Series statistics seemed to support the theory of a conspiracy.

Star pitchers Eddie Cicotte and Claude Williams lost 5 games and won only one contest.

First baseman Chick Gandil collected only 7 hits in 30 at bats, posting a sickly .233 batting average. However, he was second in runs batted in, with 5. Center fielder Happy Felsch had 5 hits in 26 at bats for a .192 average. He notched 3 RBIs. Swede Risberg hit a measly .080, with 2 hits in 25 at bats and no RBIs. Fred McMullin only got up twice. He collected one hit in his role as a pinch hitter. Most of the players mentioned (except McMullin, who rode the bench) committed costly errors at one time or another.

On the other hand, star second baseman Eddie Collins, the highest paid member of the White Sox, played honestly and had a terrible Series. He picked up only 7 hits in 31 at bats, hitting only .226. He drove in only a single run and also had a costly error. Catcher Ray Schalk hit .304 with 7 hits in 23 at bats and 2 RBIs.

The stars of the Series for the White Sox were hitters Buck Weaver, Joe Jackson, and pitcher Dickie Kerr. Jackson, in fact, set a World Series record with 12 hits. However, he was later accused of hitting selectively. Even though he led his team with 6 RBIs. Jackson was accused of not hitting aggressively with runners in scoring position.

The Cincinnati Reds' win of the 1919 World Series surprised many. From the beginning, there were rumors that the contest had been rigged.

Team owner Charles Comiskey believed some of his ballplayers had purposely not played to the best of their ability.

"There are seven boys who will never play for me again," Comiskey told reporter Fullerton in his office after the Series concluded.[6] (Exactly which seven players he was referring to was not clear. He was obviously excluding either Buck Weaver or Shoeless Joe Jackson).

Charles Comiskey was so angered by rumors of bribery that he offered a $20,000 reward to anyone who could and would provide factual evidence of a fix. The reward was written up in newspapers around the country.

Final Payoff

After the Series ended, Sport Sullivan and Brown (Nat Evans) met with Chick Gandil, Swede Risberg, and Fred McMullin. Sullivan and Brown brought with them the $40,000 that had been stored in a safe in the Hotel Congress in Chicago. The final payoff from Arnold Rothstein was handed over to Chick Gandil. Gandil gave $15,000 of the $40,000 to Swede Risberg. Risberg kept $10,000 and gave $5,000 to Fred McMullin. Chick Gandil kept the remainder of the money for himself.

Gandil made the tidy sum of $35,000 for his part in fixing the 1919 World Series. That was in addition to the money he won wagering on the Series. Hal Chase had also fared well thanks to Gandil's efforts. Chase won $40,000 on personal wagers. Joe "Sport" Sullivan was another big winner. He pocketed $50,000 in winnings. The biggest winner of all was Arnold Rothstein. Rothstein had bet $270,000 on the Cincinnati Reds to take the Series. His winnings were astronomical.

The Woes of Shoeless Joe

Joe Jackson was a very unhappy man after the 1919 World Series. He had an envelope with $5,000 in it. It had been tossed into his hotel room before Game Four of the Series by his friend Lefty Williams. Jackson took the envelope to the office of the owner of the Chicago White Sox, Charles A. Comiskey.

Comiskey's secretary, Harry Grabiner, told Jackson that he could not see the team owner. Jackson waited several hours outside of Comiskey's office and then finally gave up and left. Joe packed up his belongings, including the money, and went home to his wife.

Some sports historians speculate that Comiskey refused to see Jackson because he wanted to protect himself. Perhaps he felt rumors of the fix would blow over. Comiskey's ad asking for information about the fix continued to run in newspapers, although the amount of the reward was later reduced to $10,000.

Several people attempted to claim the reward. Joe Jackson even had his wife, Katie, write a letter to Charles Comiskey about the role gambling played in the outcome of the 1919 World Series. Charles Comiskey never answered Jackson's letter or even acknowledged it in any way. He also never paid the reward. Perhaps he hoped that all the hubbub would die down before the next baseball season. It did not. Newspapers refused to let the issue fade from public view. The worst was still yet to come. Baseball was preparing to weather a scandalous storm.

chapter five

THREE STRIKES, YOU'RE OUT!

HIGHS AND LOWS—The 1920 major-league baseball season was a year of cheers, heroics, and tragedy. The season saw a new ball introduced to the game, which gave batters an advantage. The new ball went farther when hit and helped popularize home-run hitters. Most fans agree that there is nothing more exciting than seeing a long hit clear the fences. The spitball was finally outlawed, making it illegal for pitchers to wet the ball with spit to make it curve sharply when thrown. The new emphasis in baseball was on hitting, especially home-run hitting.

Baseball fans cheered the slugging feats of Babe Ruth, the sport's new home-run king. Ruth was traded from the Boston Red Sox to the New York Yankees and astounded the sports world by clouting 54 home runs that season. The fans also cheered George Sisler of the St. Louis Browns, who topped all American League batters that season with an amazing .408 batting average. Sisler replaced Ty Cobb of the Detroit Tigers as the American League batting champion. Cobb, who had captured the title three years in a row prior to 1920, hit .334 in 1920. Fans were also thrilled by the athletic exploits of the National League's Brooklyn Dodgers. The Dodgers, led by hitter Zack Wheat and pitcher Burleigh Grimes, won the NL pennant in 1920.

The year 1920 was also a year of tragedy in baseball. In August, New York Yankee pitcher Carl Mays hit batter Ray Chapman of the Cleveland Indians in the head during a game. Chapman collapsed at the plate and later died. It was the first and only fatality in the history of major-league baseball.[1]

A tragedy of another kind began to unfold in late August 1920. Talk of the 1919 World Series fix had continued throughout the following year. More and more incidents of gambling were being reported during the 1920 season.

Some incidents were discreetly kept out of the public eye. For example, at the conclusion of the 1919 season, three National League players—Hal Chase and Heinie Zimmerman (of the New York Giants) and Lee Magee (of the Chicago Cubs, Cincinnati Reds, and Brooklyn Dodgers)—had been quietly banned from baseball for throwing games.[2]

Around that same time, Charles Comiskey hired a private detective to check up on Eddie Cicotte, Arnold Gandil, Charles Risberg, Oscar Felsch, Claude Williams, Fred McMullin, and Joe Jackson. Of those seven men, only six returned to play for the White Sox in 1920. Chick Gandil did not return. Gandil no longer needed to play baseball for a living. The detective reported that Gandil had recently purchased a new car, a new home, and lots of jewelry. Gandil's vast funds could not be explained. The money seemed to materialize out of thin air. The investigator's report supported Comiskey's suspicions of a fix the year before. However, the owner of the White Sox did not make the detective's report public. Comiskey kept silent about it. He remained quiet even when writer Hugh Fullerton asked this poignant question in the sports section of a major New York City newspaper: "Is Big League Baseball Being Run for Gamblers, with Ballplayers in the Deal?"[3]

A game that had no impact on the league standings between the fifth-place Chicago Cubs and the eighth-place Philadelphia Phillies on August 31, 1920, answered Fullerton's question.[4] The underdog Phillies won the game, 5–0. On September 4, 1920, President Bill Veeck, Sr., of the Chicago Cubs told newspapermen he had received phone calls and telegrams before the August 31 game stating that the contest had been rigged for the Cubs to lose. A Detroit gambling ring had paid players to have the game fixed. Three days later an announcement was made without much fanfare stating that the Cubs-Phillies contest would be investigated by a special Cook County, Illinois, grand jury convened to investigate major-league baseball. It was the first time that a group outside baseball checked up on the honesty of the game. The goal of the investigation was to shed light on the role gambling played in the outcome of

At age twenty-five, Charles "Swede" Risberg was the youngest of the conspirators. A close friend of Chick Gandil, Risberg was called "a hard guy" by Joe Jackson.

pro baseball games. Team owners and major-league baseball officials would not judge themselves this time. Players who were suspected of dishonest dealings would have to explain their actions to a grand jury.

The Law Steps In

The Cook County grand jury would seek the answers to questions Hugh Fullerton and other big-name sports reporters had been asking for months. Judge Charles MacDonald would preside. Harry W. Brigham, a well-known business executive, acted as jury foreman. District Attorneys Maclay Hoyne and Robert Crowe conducted the case. They were assisted by Assistant District Attorney (DA) Hartley Replogle. Replogle handled most of the work in the courtroom. He questioned the players, took statements, conducted meetings, and appeared before the press as a spokesperson.

The first witness in the case involving the Chicago Cubs was Byron Banfield Johnson, the president of the American League. Ban Johnson had long since reversed his thinking about the 1919 World Series. Over the months, he became convinced that some Chicago White Sox players had been paid to lose the 1919 World Series. He also still harbored a deep hatred of his old rival, Charles A. Comiskey. When Johnson was summoned before the Cook County grand jury to testify about the Cubs-Phillies fix, he raised the issue of the 1919 World Series results. He suggested looking into possible corruption on the part of the Chicago White Sox players the year before. Since Johnson's accusations involved a World Series crown, the grand jury paid heed to his words.

After all, the World Series was a high-profile contest certain to get major attention in the press. The Cook County grand jury quickly expanded its focus to include the 1919 World Series and the Chicago White Sox in their inquiries into gambling in baseball. After the topic of a crooked World Series was raised, the Cubs-Phillies game quickly became a minor afterthought. In fact, it was totally overlooked in the investigation and proceedings that followed.

On September 21, 1920, Assistant DA Hartley Replogle announced to the press that subpoenas had been sent out to numerous baseball players, managers, and team owners. (A subpoena is a document commanding the appearance of a witness or piece of evidence in court.) Also included in the list to testify were sportswriters and known gamblers. Hartley Replogle wanted to learn the truth about the 1919 World Series. Was the Series fixed? If it was, Assistant DA Replogle wanted to take the guilty parties before a judge in a court of law.

While the Cook County grand jury was meeting, major-league baseball games were still being played. The Brooklyn Dodgers and New York Giants were battling for first place in the National League. The defending world champion Cincinnati Reds were in third place. However, it was the pennant race in the American League that attracted the most attention. The Chicago White Sox and the Cleveland Indians were involved in a heated contest for first place. The AL pennant race became an issue in the investigation of the grand jury. So did the ongoing conflict between Ban Johnson and Charles Comiskey.

The first chief witnesses called before the grand jury were Ban Johnson, Charles Weeghman (the former owner of the Chicago Cubs), Charles Comiskey, and Rube Benton, a pitcher for the New York Giants.

After going before the grand jury, Ban Johnson was asked about his testimony by reporters. He replied, "My testimony indicated the throwing of games by several White Sox players."[5]

Johnson's statement enraged Comiskey. He accused Johnson of pointing the finger of guilt at Comiskey's players because he had personal financial interests in the Cleveland Indians. He hinted that Johnson was trying to discredit the White Sox in an effort to help the Indians in the pennant race of 1920.

"If any of my players are not honest, I'll fire them no matter who they are, and if I can't get honest players to fill their places, I'll close the gates to the park," vowed an angry Charles Comiskey.[6]

Charles Weeghman testified that one of his friends, gambler Monte Tennes, told him before the 1919 World Series that the outcome was arranged. Tennes's information was said to come directly from Abe "The Little Champ" Attell. The grand jury was informed that Attell was an associate of big-time gambler Arnold Rothstein.

One of the strongest and most important witnesses to testify was New York Giants pitcher Rube Benton. Benton was known by several names—John Cleveland Benton, Jon Calhoun Benton, and plain old Rube Benton.[7]

Benton claimed that he had been offered bribes by Hal Chase to throw games in the past. He also claimed to have seen a telegram stating that the 1919 World Series was fixed before play began. Rube Benton swore that Hal Chase and Sleepy Bill Burns were involved in the fixing of the Series. He went on to name Chick Gandil, Happy Felsch, Lefty Williams, and Eddie Cicotte as players involved in the scandal. He finished his testimony by suggesting that Cicotte be brought in for questioning.

Media Pressure

The grand jury investigation of the 1919 World Series was big news. The story received headlines in newspapers all over America. Charges of corruption were leveled at Chicago players at every turn. They appeared in newspapers. They were on the radio. Fans at games asked White Sox players on the field if the rumors were true. The only player willing to respond to the charges publicly was catcher Ray Schalk.

"It is up to baseball players themselves to protect the sport," Schalk said.[8] He was eager to go before the grand jury and promised to name guilty players. However, he was not called upon to testify.

Slowly but surely, other names and facts were uncovered by Assistant DA Hartley Replogle. A mysterious Mr. Brown was described as a hired tough guy and courier of bribe money. His part in the fix was examined by the grand

Fred McMullin, a utility infielder, was part of the plan to fix the Series only because he overheard Gandil and Risberg talking about it and forced them to include him.

jury. Arnold "Chick" Gandil was named as the ringleader of the players' conspiracy. Fred McMullin, Swede Risberg, Buck Weaver, Shoeless Joe Jackson, Happy Felsch, Lefty Williams, and Eddie Cicotte were also named as conspirators in the fix of the 1919 World Series. The press began to refer to those eight players as "The Chicago Black Sox."

On September 27, 1920, the Philadelphia *North American* newspaper featured an article that questioned the integrity of major-league baseball contests. The newspaper's headline read: "THE MOST GIGANTIC SPORTING SWINDLE IN THE HISTORY OF AMERICA."[9]

The article was an in-depth interview with small-time gambler Billy Maharg. In his interview, Maharg told all he knew about the fixing of the 1919 World Series. The story enraged baseball fans everywhere. Baseball, the game known as "America's favorite pastime," was not completely honest. Games had been fixed by gamblers and crooked players.

There was no longer any doubt in the minds of the public or the members of the grand jury. Assistant DA Hartley Replogle promised to seek indictments against the guilty parties. The men involved in the fixing of the 1919 World Series would face criminal charges in a court of law.

Players Are Suspended

The uproar over the fixing of the 1919 World Series occurred at a time when the Chicago White Sox were involved in a hotly contested pennant race in the American

League. The White Sox would need the help of all of their top athletes to win another American League crown. The defending American League champs were already without the services of Chick Gandil, who had retired at the end of the season. However, six of the other players involved in the scandal were still starters for Chicago. Nevertheless, White Sox owner Charles Comiskey suspended those six starters and a reserve player from the team. It was a gutsy move, considering that the White Sox were a much weaker team without them. The letter Comiskey sent to those players notifying them of their suspensions read as follows:

Chicago, Sept. 26

To Charles Risberg, Fred McMullin, Joe Jackson, Oscar Felsch, George Weaver, C.P. Williams and Eddie Cicotte:

You and each of you are hereby notified of your indefinite suspension as a member of the Chicago American League Baseball Club.

Your suspension is brought about by information which has just come to me directly involving you and each of you in the baseball scandal resulting from the world's series of 1919.

If you are innocent of any wrongdoing you and each of you will be reinstated; if you are guilty you will be retired from organized baseball for the rest of your lives if I can accomplish it.

Until there is a finality to this investigation it is due to the public that I take this action, even though it costs Chicago the pennant.

Chicago America Baseball Club
By Charles A. Comiskey[10]

White Sox pitcher Eddie Cicotte was ready to appear before the grand jury. Cicotte was very anxious about the outcome of that upcoming appearance. Before he faced the grand jury, a nervous Cicotte had a meeting with team owner Charles A. Comiskey, manager Kid Gleason, and Comiskey's attorney, Alfred Austrian. Cicotte was so upset he blurted out a tearful confession to the White Sox owner.

"I don't know what you'll think of me," Cicotte told Comiskey, "but I got to tell you how I double-crossed you. Mr. Comiskey, I did double-cross you. I'm a crook, and I got $10,000 for being a crook."[11]

Charles Comiskey was repulsed by Cicotte's admission of guilt. He had little sympathy for his former star.

"Don't tell it to me," snapped Comiskey, "tell it to the judge!"[12]

The Grand Jury

Eddie Cicotte went before the grand jury and told of his involvement in the fix. Cicotte made no excuses for his guilt.

"I never did anything I regretted as much in my life," said Cicotte after a meeting with Judge Charles MacDonald before testifying to the grand jury. "I would give anything in the world if I could undo my acts in the last world's series. I've played a crooked game and I have lost, and I am here to tell the whole truth."[13]

Joe Jackson, the next White Sox player to appear before the grand jury, was also very nervous and eager to clear his name of any wrongdoing. In addition, Jackson sought public forgiveness for his part in the scheme. However, Jackson's actual involvement in the conspiracy is difficult to determine even to this day. Many of his comments are confusing and contradictory. Even though he claimed he was innocent, his own words sometimes made him sound guilty.

"I got a big load off of my chest," Jackson later said. "I'm feeling better."[14]

The statement makes it sound like Jackson was involved. Later, Joe claims he was merely an innocent pawn and never actually participated in any phase of the fix.

George "Buck" Weaver made his position clear from the outset. He declared his total innocence. Buck admitted to sitting in on two meetings with the conspirators but insisted he did nothing wrong or illegal. Weaver said that he had played hard and had received no money. His World Series statistics seemed to bear out his claim. Weaver, Jackson, and Dickie Kerr were the stars for Chicago in the 1919 World Series.

Oscar "Happy" Felsch and Claude "Lefty" Williams followed Cicotte's example and admitted to their roles in the fixing of the 1919 World Series. Both men were willing to accept the consequences of their actions. Cicotte, Felsch, and Williams signed confessions that detailed their involvement in the scheme. In his confession, Lefty Williams named Sport Sullivan and a man named Brown as playing key roles in the gambling scheme. Joe Jackson also signed a confession. In it, however, Jackson did not admit that he had played poorly for pay. He just admitted to being involved.

Arnold "Chick" Gandil, Charles "Swede" Risberg, and Fred McMullin all stayed tight-lipped. They refused to admit any guilt. In fact, they denied having any involvement at all in a fix.

Building a Case

Assistant District Attorney Replogle began to build a criminal case based on the testimony of witnesses who had appeared before the grand jury.

One witness was Henrietta Kelly, the owner of an apartment house where many of the White Sox players lived during the season. Kelly claimed to have overheard Eddie Cicotte speaking on the telephone with his brother before the 1919 World Series. She testified that Cicotte had told his brother that the Series was fixed.

Several major-league managers and players, some of whom won money betting on the 1919 World Series, also appeared before the grand jury. The most damaging testimony of all came from several of the White Sox players who were involved in the scheme. It was their willingness to admit guilt that placed them in jeopardy.

Eddie Cicotte was boldly frank before the grand jury. He held nothing back and revealed in detail how he had assisted the opposition in winning the first and fourth games of the World Series. His statements were written up, and the confession was signed by Cicotte. As stated earlier, Lefty Williams also told all he knew about the scheme and signed a confession. An important part of Williams's confession detailed the involvement of his friend, Joe Jackson, in the

Lefty Williams, like Eddie Cicotte and Joe Jackson, admitted to his participation in the scheme and signed a confession.

fixing scheme. Lefty Williams swore that Shoeless Joe Jackson never willingly accepted any bribe money. The money had been forced on him.

Joe Jackson, too, signed a confession. The validity of that confession remains in question to this day. Jackson could barely read or write. The confession he signed was prepared for him by Alfred Austrian. Austrian was an attorney for the Chicago White Sox and was on the payroll of team owner Charles Comiskey. Did Shoeless Joe Jackson really know what he was signing? Did Austrian have the welfare of Joe Jackson in mind when he prepared the confession, or was he more concerned with protecting the image of the White Sox team? The answers to those questions are not known.

What is known is that Joe Jackson later claimed that he had never read his own confession. Over the years, there has been speculation that Alfred Austrian misled Jackson in order to protect the reputation of his longtime client, Charles Comiskey.

Joe Jackson's confession stated that the star outfielder sat in on meetings held by the conspirators. Jackson knew a fix was in the works but did not immediately report what he knew to White Sox manager Kid Gleason or team owner Charles Comiskey. Furthermore, Jackson admitted that Lefty Williams had given him five thousand dollars in cash. Jackson did not admit to playing poorly for the money. There was no evidence to suggest that he did. The worst Shoeless Joe could be accused of concerning his play was not delivering key hits when the team needed them. Jackson had failed to connect for important hits when runners were in scoring position during the 1919 World Series.

"I can say that my conscience is clear," Jackson later said about the 1919 World Series. "Let the Lord be my judge."[15]

DA Hartley Replogle was more than satisfied with Jackson's testimony before the grand jury. He even seemed to want to protect Joe from the press.

"Don't ask Joe any questions," Replogle told reporters after Jackson spent two hours talking about the fix. "He's gone through beautifully and we don't want him bothered."[16]

While Cicotte, Williams, and Jackson made and signed confessions before the grand jury, Oscar "Happy" Felsch did not. He did submit a signed confession, but it was not to the grand jury. Felsch prepared a confession and issued it as a statement to the press. In the statement, Felsch admitted to his involvement in the scheme.

The players, Henrietta Kelly, and baseball officials were not the only individuals to appear before the grand jury. Gamblers Bill Burns, Billy Maharg, Sport Sullivan, Abe Attell, and Arnold Rothstein were also summoned. Burns and Maharg proved to be very talkative. The two small-time gamblers revealed everything they knew. They explained in detail their parts in the scheme. Sport Sullivan also talked and tried to shift the blame for the fix from himself to Arnold Rothstein. He named Rothstein as a principal force in the fixing of the 1919 World Series. Abe Attell did not implicate Rothstein.

Arnold "The Big Bankroll" Rothstein lived up to his image as a wealthy man of the world. He arranged things so he was permitted to have an attorney present when he was questioned. That attorney was a well-known, high-priced New York lawyer named William Fallon. In front of the grand jury, Arnold Rothstein strongly denied having any involvement in the fixing of the 1919 World Series. He also contested the story of Billy Maharg that had appeared in the newspapers. Rothstein swore he was innocent and placed the blame, if there was any to be placed, on his friend Abe Attell.

The grand jury could not prove or disprove the claims of Arnold Rothstein. There was no evidence to connect him directly to the fixing of the 1919 World Series. Rothstein walked away from the hearing knowing he could not be prosecuted. Indeed, he was not.

When the grand jury concluded its investigation, there were legal grounds for a trial. The evidence was strong enough against the Chicago Black Sox, as they were called by the press, to take the case to court. There were many people involved in the fixing of the 1919 World Series. Not all of them would stand trial in court. Some would receive immunity from prosecution in exchange for their testimony. Others would leave Chicago and fight legal battles against being extradited (sent from one state to another to appear in court). The eight Chicago Black Sox would stand trial in a court of law. It was the players who were mainly held accountable for the sports disgrace of the century. Eddie Cicotte, Joe Jackson, Oscar Felsch, Claude Williams, Arnold Gandil, Charles Risberg, Fred McMullin, and George Weaver were indicted. Also indicted were Abe Attell, Hal Chase, Joseph Sullivan, Bill Burns, Nat Evans ("Mr. Brown"), David Zelser, Carl Zork, Benjamin Franklin, Rachael Brown, Lou Levi, and his brother Ben Levi. The

Levi brothers, Brown, Franklin, Zork, and Zelser became involved in the scheme when Abe Attell needed money to pay the players. They were the partners Attell had told Burns and Billy Maharg about when the gamblers all met in the hotel before the 1919 World Series.

Baseball's Response

Shortly after the White Sox players were indicted, Charles Comiskey and Alfred Austrian began to distance themselves

Oscar "Happy" Felsch presented his confession as a statement to the press rather than the grand jury. He later told author Eliot Asinof, "There was so much crookedness around, you sort of fell into it."

from their corrupt players. At the time of the indictments, Austrian told reporters:

> Mr. Comiskey and myself, as his counsel, have been working on this for a year. We have spent a great deal of Mr. Comiskey's money to ferret it out. It is because of our investigation the lid has been blown off this scandal.[17]

The White Sox team could not keep pace with the Cleveland Indians in the American League pennant race without the services of its missing players. The Indians passed the White Sox in the standings and maintained their lead until the season ended. Cleveland took the American League pennant with a record of 98 wins and 56 losses. The White Sox placed second, with a record of 96 wins and 58 losses. The Indians then went on to top the Brooklyn Dodgers in the World Series, 5 games to 2. Thanks to the scandal of 1919, the White Sox dynasty was destroyed. It would take many years of rebuilding to once again become a championship contender.

At the end of the 1920 baseball season, team owners decided that pro baseball had to be cleaned up if was to survive as a fan favorite. It was decided that the three-man National Commission that had governed baseball up to that time should be disbanded. It would be replaced by a single, independent commissioner with ultimate decision-making power over all aspects of pro baseball. The commissioner's job would be to render decisions in the best interests of baseball—giving him vague but complete authority over the team owners, players, managers, and umpires.

The baseball team owners selected as their first commissioner a judge who had gained national prominence for a daring act: He attempted to extradite Kaiser Wilhelm of Germany to the United States to stand trial for the sinking of the *Lusitania,* an American passenger ship that had been sunk by a German submarine. Many Americans were killed in the sinking, and it was one of the main reasons for the United States entry into World War I. The name of that fearless judge was Kenesaw Mountain Landis.

Landis knew the sport of baseball. As a judge, he had ruled in favor of the American and National leagues in an antitrust suit when a new competitor, called the Federal League, tried to raid the majors of their best players. (The Federal League later collapsed financially.)

When the search for a commissioner began, American folk storyteller and comedian Will Rogers had this to say about Landis's possible appointment: "Somebody said, get that old boy who sits behind first base all the time. He's out there every day anyhow, so they offered him a season's pass and he jumped at it."[18] Rogers joked about the appointment, but he believed Landis was a good choice for the position.

However, not everyone considered Kenesaw Mountain Landis the perfect man to fill the job of baseball commissioner. Some people believed him to be overdramatic and a publicity hound. "His career typifies the heights to which dramatic talent may carry a man in America if only he has the foresight not to go onto the stage," said Heywood Broun, one of the most influential newspaper columnists of the time.[19]

The Black Sox Are Arraigned

Judge William Dever presided over the arraignment of the Black Sox players on February 14, 1921. (People arraigned are called into court to answer formal charges made in an indictment.) In charge of the case for the prosecution was George Gorman, a famous attorney. Gorman had quietly confessed to his associates that he had little hope of winning the case. He did not feel the evidence was solid enough. Gorman was assisted by Anthony E. Prindeville. At the arraignment, Thomas Nash, the counsel for Buck Weaver, moved to have a separate trial for his client. The motion was denied because Weaver had been indicted for conspiracy and had to stand trial with his fellow conspirators. (A conspiracy is when two or more people plan together to injure an individual or to do other unlawful acts.)

Of those seven conspirators, Fred McMullin was the only one originally indicted by the grand jury who never actually went to trial. The prosecution deemed the case against McMullin too weak.[20] Perhaps the fact that McMullin had played in only two games of the 1919 World Series—coming to bat twice as a pinch hitter and getting only one hit—had something to do with the prosecutor's decision. McMullin really played no role—positive or negative—in the outcome of the 1919 World Series.

Before the trial began, Joe Jackson, Claude Williams, and Eddie Cicotte all claimed their confessions were not valid. Jackson insisted his confession was untrue because he had never read the confession prior to signing it (or had any-one explain it to him).

The players also raised a question about immunity from prosecution. The players said they had been promised that they would be immune to legal prosecution if they signed the confessions. They believed that justice had failed them.

In a way, justice had failed in the case. Fred McMullin and Arnold Rothstein were not the only ones connected with the 1919 World Series fixing who escaped prosecution. Prior to the trial, Abe Attell was arrested in New York on a minor charge. Attell was in jail and while there waged a legal battle to keep New York authorities from turning him over to Illinois officials so he could stand trial in Chicago. Attell's lawyer was Bill Fallon, who also had Arnold Rothstein for a client. Fallon argued that the Attell under arrest in New York was not the same Abe Attell who was wanted in Chicago and therefore should not be extradited to Illinois. It was a crafty legal maneuver. New York magistrate Robert C. Teneyeck decided that there was insufficient evidence to cause Attell's extradition. Abe "The Little Champ" Attell did not return to Chicago to stand trial.

Joe "Sport" Sullivan slipped out of the United States and moved to Quebec, Canada. He, too, escaped extradition and did not stand trial for fixing the 1919 World Series. Another one of the gamblers, Rachael Brown, simply vanished. He was not found. California refused to extradite Hal Chase, who was a native son of the state. Chase also escaped prosecution. Gambler Bill Burns left Chicago and returned to Texas.

The Black Sox conspirators and their attorneys are shown in court. The players who conspired to fix the game were tried, but the big-time gamblers associated with the fix were never brought to court.

Byron Banfield Johnson, who was determined to see the case prosecuted, knew the prosecution was in dire need of witnesses and decided to help find them. Johnson helped the prosecution make a deal with Billy Maharg. Johnson then enlisted the help of Maharg in tracking down his old comrade, Sleepy Bill Burns. Burns was located in a remote area of Texas. Both Maharg and Burns were promised immunity to testify in the case. They agreed to do it.

On June 27, 1921, the trial of what was now the Chicago Black Sox Seven began. The presiding judge was Hugo Friend. The charges against the seven players were as follows:

1. A conspiracy to defraud the public

2. A conspiracy to defraud Ray Schalk

3. A conspiracy to commit a confidence game

4. A conspiracy to injure the business of the American League

5. A conspiracy to injure the business of Charles A. Comiskey

(To defraud means to obtain money under false circumstances or promises. A confidence game is a phony way to get money from someone. Today it might be called a con game.)

The defense team included lawyers Ben Short, Michael Ahearn, Thomas Nash, and James O'Brien, who had formerly been a legal associate of Alfred Austrian, Charles Comiskey's team attorney. When O'Brien became part of the defense team, it suggested to those following the case that Charles Comiskey wanted his players to be found not guilty, even though he himself was a witness for the prosecution.

Max Luster and A. Morgan Frumberg were the attorneys for the remaining gamblers who were on hand to stand trial: Carl Zork, David Zelser, Benjamin Franklin, Lou and Ben Levi, and Nat Evans ("Mr. Brown").

The Jury and Witnesses

Over six hundred prospective jurors were questioned before the actual trial began. Some were challenged by the prosecution and dismissed. Others were challenged by the defense and dismissed. Because of the massive press coverage of the case, it was difficult to find potential jurors who had not already made up their minds about the guilt or innocence of the individuals involved. It took until July 15, 1921, to secure a jury satisfactory to both the prosecution and the defense. The jury was composed entirely of men. Most were blue-collar workers.

The first witness for the prosecution was Charles A. Comiskey. Comiskey's testimony did not really help the prosecution. Ben Short, an attorney for the defense, used his cross-examination to portray the team owner as a man obsessed with self-promotion. Short's questions made Charles Comiskey seem like a man who only cared about making money for himself. He did not appear to be a crusader for honest play in baseball.

The next witness was gambler Bill Burns, who had been granted immunity from prosecution in exchange for his testimony. Burns told his story of the fix under the guided questioning of Assistant Prosecutor Anthony Prindeville. Bill Burns was the prosecution's key witness. He remained on the witness stand for several days. He was questioned by Prindeville and State's Attorney George Gorman. Burns was also closely cross-examined by defense attorney Michael Ahearn, who realized how important Burns was. The case for the prosecution hinged on the testimony of Sleepy Bill Burns.

On July 22, 1921, an event occurred that affected the outcome of the case. State's Attorney George Gorman advised Judge Hugo Friend that the signed confessions of Eddie Cicotte, Claude Williams, and Joe Jackson had mysteriously vanished from the court files and were presumed to have been stolen from the prosecutor's office. (Happy Felsch's confession had been given to the press, not to the grand jury, and was not on file.) Gorman stated that he himself had never seen the confessions. He did not know what had happened to the originals. Carbon copies did exist, but they were not signed by the players. Judge Friend ruled that unless the State could prove that the confessions were made voluntarily, they could not be entered into the trial. An argument erupted between the prosecuting and defense attorneys about whether or not the confessions were voluntary. After some intense questioning of Cicotte and Jackson, Judge Friend ruled that their confessions were indeed voluntary.

Weak Evidence and a Quick Verdict

The court case against Joe Jackson, Eddie Cicotte, Buck Weaver, Swede Risberg, Lefty Williams, Happy Felsch, and Chick Gandil dragged on until August 2, 1921.

The evidence presented by the prosecution was weak and incomplete at best. The confessions signed by Eddie Cicotte, Joe Jackson, and Claude Williams had vanished. All that remained were unsigned carbon copies. Members of the grand jury, court clerks, and stenographers could testify to having heard and seen the original confessions, but the players all claimed the confessions were not valid.

Several key people never took the stand as witnesses. Abe Attell, Sport Sullivan, and Arnold Rothstein never testified.

Bill Burns and Billy Maharg did testify in court. The two small-time gamblers accused famous and popular players of wrongdoing. In the eyes of the jury, it was a question of which men were more believable. Sleepy Bill Burns was the key to the case for the prosecution. He placed the burden of guilt on Gandil, Risberg, Felsch, Williams, and Cicotte. He had never spoken directly to Jackson, and McMullin was not on trial.

To many sports fans following the case, it seemed that the baseball players were being targeted more than the gam-

blers, who had gained the most from the fix. The State was asking for a sentence of five years in jail and a $2,000 fine for each of the Chicago players involved in the scandal. The big-time gamblers—Arnold Rothstein, Abe Attell, and Sport Sullivan—never even made it to trial. It was those gamblers who benefited most from the fix, yet they got off scot-free.

"Sleepy" Bill Burns, a former pro baseball player (shown here in a Chicago uniform), was one of the gamblers involved in fixing the series.

The question the jury had to consider was, How would justice best be served?

Public sentiment was also now with the players. Joe Jackson and Buck Weaver were being hailed as tragic figures caught in a web of corruption. Eddie Cicotte, Lefty Williams, and Oscar Felsch were pitied by many who thought they were underpaid by a rich team owner. Blue-collar Americans saw the players as pawns used by Charles Comiskey to increase his personal wealth. And then there were Chick Gandil and Swede Risberg, who still adamantly denied any guilt at all.

It took the jury just two hours and forty-seven minutes to reach a decision. All of the defendants were found not guilty. Judge Hugo Friend agreed with the verdict. Judge Friend contended that the not-guilty verdict was a direct result of insufficient evidence presented by the prosecution. Prosecutor George Gorman's earlier feelings that the case against the players could not be won had proved accurate.

"I knew I'd be cleared. And I'm glad the public stood by me until the trial was over," said Buck Weaver.[21]

"I guess that'll learn [AL President] Ban Johnson he can't frame an honest bunch of ballplayers," cheered Chick Gandil.[22]

The Chicago Black Sox had washed their dirty laundry in public and came out of the ordeal legally clean. The players staged a huge celebration after the verdict was announced. However, their joy and exhilaration were short-lived.

chapter six

JUDGMENT DAY AT THE BALLPARK

FINAL VERDICT—"It has been said of the 1919 'Black Sox' scandal . . . that it signified an end to American innocence," wrote James Mote, an expert on baseball, some seventy years after the big fix.[1]

Perhaps it was not so much an end to innocence as an end to the public's ignorance of the shortcomings of pro sports and the wrongdoing of athletes who play for pay. When the scandal was finally revealed, the people in charge of major-league baseball could no longer just look the other way. Something had to be done to rescue the integrity of professional baseball. Fans of the sport had to be certain the outcomes of games were not predetermined.

Baseball commissioner Kenesaw Mountain Landis realized those facts as he watched the trial of the Black Sox players. Landis, himself a federal judge, knew that he had a difficult decision to make. Even though all seven members of the White Sox were found not guilty in a courtroom, there would always be some fans who still questioned

Judge Kenesaw Mountain Landis, the first commissioner of baseball, had to deal with the baseball scandal of 1919. His decision to bar the players from baseball for life has been called extremely unfair by some; others have credited him with saving the sport.

the players' real involvement in the incident. Had they accepted bribes? Had they played poorly on purpose? Had they gotten away with throwing the World Series because of a lack of evidence?

Landis also had to consider the standard set by the court case. Would other pro baseball players be tempted to accept bribes because they did not fear being punished? Commissioner Landis decided to make an example of the Chicago Black Sox. His punishment would be stern and unyielding. But was the punishment fair? You will have to decide that for yourself.

After they were cleared in court, White Sox players believed that their troubles were over. Joe Jackson and Buck Weaver were anxious to return to the game they loved to play. Weaver had offers from several other major-league teams interested in signing him on for the next season.

On the south side of Chicago, a petition had been circulated calling for major-league baseball to reinstate Buck Weaver. In a single day, fourteen thousand baseball fans had signed the petition.

Joe Jackson was also eager to return to baseball. He expected to be instantly reinstated. Jackson figured that he would be playing ball for the White Sox once again. He was wrong.

On August 3, 1921, the day after the not-guilty verdict was announced, baseball commissioner Kenesaw Mountain Landis released a statement that shattered the baseball dreams of Buck Weaver and Joe Jackson forever. He wrote:

> Regardless of the verdict of juries, no player that throws a ball game, no player that entertains proposals or promises to throw a game, no player that sits in a conference with a bunch of crooked players and gamblers where the ways and means of throwing games are discussed, and does not promptly tell his club about it, will ever again play professional baseball.[2]

Despite the fact that they had been acquitted in court, Chick Gandil, Swede Risberg, Fred McMullin, Lefty Williams, Happy Felsch, Eddie Cicotte, Shoeless Joe Jackson, and Buck Weaver were banned by Commissioner Landis from playing major-league baseball for life. In doing so, Landis ended three potential Hall of Fame careers in the blink of an eye. Eddie Cicotte would never pitch in another major-league baseball game. Buck Weaver would never play third base for any major-league team. Shoeless Joe Jackson, the man Ty Cobb called "the greatest pure hitter I ever saw,"[3] would never swing Black Betsy, his famous bat, and connect with the ball for another major-league hit. Their careers in the big leagues were abruptly terminated.

It is a popular American belief that the punishment should fit the crime. In the case of the eight Black Sox players, the ruling of Commissioner Landis was made based on the actions of the group rather than individuals. Landis never considered each man's degree of involvement in the fix individually. He judged them all equally guilty. Some newspapers and sportswriters of the time applauded Commissioner Landis's decision. They believed his ruling sent a stern message to pro ballplayers. It was clear that not even the slightest hint of gambling would be tolerated in major-league baseball. It was a point that had to be made to pro athletes. Gambling on games was strictly off-limits for players. But was Landis's ruling fair to Joe Jackson and Buck Weaver?

Five months after he was banned from baseball for life, Buck Weaver met with Commissioner Landis to plead for reinstatement. Once again, Weaver told the story of his limited involvement with the conspirators. Once again, Landis upheld his earlier decision. Buck Weaver received no sympathy from the commissioner. He remained banned from major-league baseball.

A Civil Case

Even though they were officially banned from playing major-league baseball, Buck Weaver and Joe Jackson still had binding three-year contracts with the Chicago White Sox in 1920. Weaver and Jackson were each due to be paid $7,500 a year by team owner Charles Comiskey. Neither player received any payment in 1921. Weaver and Jackson both took Charles Comiskey to civil court to recover their lost pay.

The legal matter of how much money, if any, Charles Comiskey owed those two players dragged on in civil courts for over three years. In 1924 a civil court finally ruled in favor of Joe Jackson, finding him not guilty of being involved in the 1919 Black Sox scandal. The court awarded Joe Jackson over $16,000 in back pay. Meanwhile, Buck Weaver agreed to an out-of-court settlement with Charles Comiskey. Weaver accepted a few thousand dollars to drop his civil suit. After the civil court found Joe Jackson innocent of any involvement in the 1919 fixing of the World Series, both Jackson and Buck Weaver again went to the baseball commissioner. The players begged to be reinstated. Landis steadfastly refused to change his decision. Jackson and Weaver remained banned for life.

Judge Kenesaw Mountain Landis is best remembered for his banishment of the Chicago Black Sox Eight. However, on other occasions he was less than successful in his dealings with baseball players accused of having gambling connections.

The case of Rogers Hornsby of the St. Louis Cardinals is a good example. Hornsby was a well-respected man off the field. He was also one of the greatest second basemen of all time. Hornsby's batting average was never less than .384. The star infielder hit over .400 three times. Baseball fans and sportswriters loved Hornsby. Rogers Hornsby's one weakness was that he had a passion for horse racing. He enjoyed placing wagers on horses, which was perfectly legal. He also knew a lot about horse racing and often gave fellow ballplayers tips on which horses to bet on.

Commissioner Landis took the position that Rogers Hornsby had a gambling habit. Landis considered Hornsby a compulsive gambler. The commissioner did not want a repeat of the 1919 incident, so he summoned Hornsby to a meeting.

Rogers Hornsby was infuriated. He knew he was doing nothing wrong. He also knew that the commissioner often dabbled in the stock market, which Hornsby considered a form of gambling. In the meeting, Landis and Hornsby argued over what was gambling and what was not. Behind closed doors, it was decided that Rogers Hornsby could bet on horse races if Commissioner Landis could play the stock market.

Rogers Hornsby was not the only star player to lock horns with Commissioner Landis after the 1919 case. Detroit's Ty Cobb and Cleveland's Tris Speaker, both Hall of Fame players, were summoned before Commissioner Landis in 1926. Hubert "Dutch" Leonard, formerly a pitcher with the Boston Red Sox and Detroit Tigers, claimed to have incriminating letters from ex-pitcher "Smokey Joe" Wood of the Boston Red Sox and Cleveland Indians. Leonard said the letters implicated Cobb and Speaker in past betting scandals.[4]

To avoid another possible public scandal, Landis tried to persuade Ty Cobb and Tris Speaker to retire quietly from major-league baseball. The two superstars refused and demanded to meet with their accuser face-to-face. When Dutch Leonard heard that Cobb and Speaker wanted to make a public issue of his charges, he became worried. For reasons unknown, Dutch Leonard refused to face Cobb and Speaker. Commissioner Landis was then forced to withdraw the charges against the two superstars. By the year 1926, the times had changed. The public had little interest in slinging mud on the good names of established sports icons without cold, hard facts to support any accusations. Of course, that new public feeling did little to help the cases of Joe Jackson and Buck Weaver, who were still banned from playing major-league baseball.

In 1924 the stolen confessions of Joe Jackson, Eddie Cicotte, and Claude Williams mysteriously reappeared in the possession of attorney George B. Hudnall, an associate of Alfred Austrian. Hudnall and Austrian both worked for Charles Comiskey.

At the time, Hudnall was representing Charles Comiskey in the civil case Joe Jackson had filed against Comiskey demanding his back pay. Jackson's attorney was a man named Raymond Cannon. Hudnall tried to use the confessions as an admission of wrongdoing on Jackson's part. It was a clever scheme on the part of Hudnall to save Comiskey from paying Jackson any money. It did not work. Comiskey still had to pay.

Of course, the sudden reappearance of the stolen confessions raised some other questions. Where did Hudnall get the confessions, which had disappeared during the trial of the Chicago Black Sox? That question was never answered. It was presumed that gangster Arnold Rothstein had the confessions stolen and later sold them to Charles Comiskey. The truth will probably never be known.

The Fates of the Gamblers

In 1921 Arnold Rothstein was still a passionate fan of the game of baseball. He established a new friendship with Charles Stoneham, the owner of the New York Giants. Rothstein was seen frequenting Stoneham's private box at the Polo Grounds Stadium in New York, where the Giants played their home games. When Commissioner Landis learned of Stoneham's public association with Rothstein, he forced the team owner of the Giants to terminate the relationship.

Later in 1921 Rothstein announced he was finished with gambling. He became involved with other types of unlawful activities, including the selling of drugs and illegal alcohol. (The manufacture and sale of alcohol were forbidden in the

United States between 1920 and 1933; this became known as the Prohibition Era.)

On November 6, 1928, Arnold Rothstein was shot in the stomach during a card game at a New York hotel. A player in the game accused Rothstein of cheating. The gunshot wound was fatal. Rothstein's murderer was never caught. At the time of his death, Arnold Rothstein was forty-six years old. He had never been convicted of a single crime.

When the Federal Bureau of Investigation went through Rothstein's files after his death, they found papers revealing that William J. Kelly, the attorney for Joseph "Sport" Sullivan, had four affidavits dealing with Rothstein's involvement in the 1919 World Series fix. There were references to payments of $80,000 to ballplayers. The affidavits were signed by Abe Attell, William Fallon, Eugene McGee (Fallon's partner), and Joseph Sullivan. Other papers showed that Rothstein had paid $53,000 to Kelly for the affidavits. After his death, Arnold "The Big Bankroll" Rothstein was finally tied to the fixing of the 1919 World Series by solid evidence. Rothstein and the other gangsters involved in the scheme were forever linked to the biggest scandal in baseball history.

Abe Attell transported illegal whiskey and operated a speakeasy (an illegal bar) during Prohibition. He was arrested many times but never committed a major crime. In 1961, at the age of seventy-eight, Attell issued a public statement about his involvement in the 1919 World Series scandal. Attell claimed to be innocent of any wrongdoing and placed all blame on Arnold Rothstein.

Bill Burns, Billy Maharg, Hal Chase, Joseph "Sport" Sullivan, and the other gamblers involved in the 1919 big fix went on to lead reasonably obscure lives. Some were involved in other small-time betting schemes, but they never resurfaced as major forces in the world of crime.

Others Involved in the Case

Judge Kenesaw Mountain Landis remained as baseball commissioner from his appointment in 1920 until his death in 1944. He was succeeded by Albert B. "Happy" Chandler, the former governor of Kentucky. For the most part, Landis is fondly remembered as the man who preserved the

Despite the scandal of the 1919 World Series, baseball gained in popularity in the years that followed. Shown is President Calvin Coolidge throwing out the first pitch of the 1924 Series between the Washington Senators and the New York Giants.

integrity of major-league baseball. He was named to the Baseball Hall of Fame in 1944.

Charles A. Comiskey was known by the nicknames "Old Roman" (because of the classical shape of his nose) and "Commy" (short for Comiskey). He spent his entire life in baseball as a player-manager and team owner.

Comiskey's players considered him a miser, but some people outside baseball considered him a philanthropist. Once he donated 10 percent of his team's 1918 gross receipts to the American Red Cross.[5] Charles Comiskey died in 1931 at the age of seventy-two. In 1939 he was elected to the Baseball Hall of Fame.

Rube Benton never became a big league fixture on the mound as a pitcher. After the trial, he spent most of his playing years in the minor leagues. In 1923, manager Pat Moran of the Cincinnati Reds wanted to bring Benton up from the minors to boost his pitching staff. National League president John Heydler tried to keep Benton from returning to the major leagues, citing his former association with gamblers. Commissioner Landis overruled Heydler, and Rube Benton joined the Reds pitching staff for part of the 1923 season.

The White Sox Players

Catcher Ray Schalk eventually became the manager of the Chicago White Sox. He also coached baseball at Purdue University. Kid Gleason quit as the team manager of the Chicago White Sox after the 1923 season and stayed out of baseball for several years. In 1926 he returned to the major leagues as a coach for Connie Mack's Philadelphia

Athletics. Eventually Kid Gleason grew old in the game of baseball and became known as "Pop" Gleason.

In 1921 pitcher Dickie Kerr won nineteen games for the Chicago White Sox. In 1922 he was involved in a contract dispute with Charles Comiskey over salary. Comiskey refused to pay what Kerr thought he was worth, so Kerr sat out the 1922 major-league season. Instead, Kerr played semipro baseball, appearing in several contests against his former Black Sox teammates.

Commissioner Landis heard about the games and declared Dickie Kerr ineligible to play major-league baseball for a year because he had associated with banned players. Dickie Kerr felt Landis's ruling was unfair but could do nothing about it.

With the exception of Chick Gandil, all of the banished Black Sox players spent some time playing semipro baseball or playing for teams unaffiliated with the major leagues, known as outlaw teams. Sometimes those players appeared on rosters using phony names.

Fred McMullin. Fred McMullin played some semipro baseball and then dropped completely out of the public eye. In 1951, he died at age sixty-one in Los Angeles, California.

Arnold "Chick" Gandil. Chick Gandil returned to California with his wife and became a plumber. He led a quiet and peaceful life, dying in 1970 at the age of eighty-two.

Charles "Swede" Risberg. Swede Risberg played semipro baseball and outlaw ball for a team known as the Black Sox. He also worked on a dairy farm in Minnesota and later ran a tavern on the Oregon border. He died in 1975 at age eighty-one in Red Bluff, California.

Claude "Lefty" Williams. Claude Williams stayed near Chicago and ran a pool hall. He then moved to Laguna Beach, California, and managed a nursery business. He died in 1955 at age sixty-six.

Oscar "Happy" Felsch. Oscar Felsch played baseball with the outlaw baseball team the Black Sox. He then moved back to Milwaukee, Wisconsin, where he ran a tavern. Felsch, a popular local figure, had six children and nine grandchildren. He died in 1964 at the age of seventy-three.

Eddie Cicotte. Eddie Cicotte worked on his farm and also worked as a game warden. He played baseball for the Black Sox outlaw team and other clubs. In 1923 he pitched in an outlaw league in Louisiana under the name of Moore. Swede Risberg was also on that team. So was an outfielder known as Johnson who in reality was Shoeless Joe Jackson. In 1969, Cicotte died in Detroit, Michigan, at the age of eighty-five.

George "Buck" Weaver. Buck Weaver never gave up hope that he would someday be reinstated and play major-league baseball again. He owned a Chicago drugstore that proved to be a successful business. Finally, in 1927, Weaver joined the semipro Mid-West League and played for a Hammond, Indiana, team. He was thirty-seven years old.

Buck Weaver died of a heart attack at age sixty-six in Chicago, Illinois, in 1956.

"Shoeless" Joe Jackson. Joe Jackson played semipro baseball and outlaw baseball. Sometimes he played under

Ty Cobb (left) and Joe Jackson, shown in this 1913 photo, were two of the game's greatest hitters. While both men tangled with Judge Kenesaw Mountain Landis over betting scandals, Cobb was never prosecuted, and he ended up in the Baseball Hall of Fame. Many people believe Joe Jackson should be there, too.

assumed names. In addition to using the name Johnson, he played for a team in Hackensack, New Jersey, under the name of Joseph. He was a great player until the end.

Jackson owned a liquor store in Greenville, South Carolina. He passed away in 1951 at age sixty-two, shortly after being inducted into the Cleveland Baseball Hall of Fame. (The Cleveland Baseball Hall of Fame honors athletes who played for teams in that city; it is not connected with the National Baseball Hall of Fame.)

Jackson never felt any remorse about his involvement in the scandal and felt no bitterness about not being eligible to enter baseball's Hall of Fame. He believed that his statistics and records spoke for the kind of player he was.

Chicago 1919 World Series Stats

Examine the following stats. Do they bear out the accusations that all the so-called "Black Sox" played poorly in the 1919 World Series? Be sure to compare the stats of the accused players with the stats of those *not* involved in the scandal. For example, Eddie Collins, a star infielder who was not implicated in the fix, played very poorly. His statistics paled when compared to the stats of Joe Jackson and Buck Weaver, who ended up banished from baseball for life. Even Ray Schalk, who loudly condemned the play of his "crooked" teammates, collected only 7 hits—as did Chick Gandil, who played badly on purpose.

The pitching stats also need to be looked at. Other than Dickie Kerr's 1.42 earned run average, most of the statistics are about equal; the entire pitching staff performed badly.

BATTING

NAME	GAMES	POS.	AB	R	HITS	2B	3B	HR	RBI	BA
"Black" Sox										
Weaver	8	3B	34	4	11	4	1	0	0	.324
Jackson	8	LF	32	5	12	3	0	1	6	.375
Gandil	8	1B	30	1	7	0	1	0	5	.233
Felsch	8	CF	26	2	5	1	0	0	3	.192
Risberg	8	SS	25	3	2	0	1	0	0	.080
McMullin	8	PH	2	0	1	0	0	0	0	.500
"Clean" White Sox										
E. Collins	8	2B	31	2	7	1	0	0	1	.226
Schalk	8	C	23	1	7	0	0	0	2	.304
Leibold	5	RF	18	0	1	0	0	0	0	.056
S. Collins	4	RF	16	2	4	1	0	0	0	.250

NOTE: AB = at bats; R = runs; 2B = hit double; 3B = hit triple;
HR = home run; RBI = runs batted in; BA = batting average.

PITCHING

NAME	GAMES	INNINGS PITCHED	HITS	BB	SO	ERA
"Black Sox"						
Cicotte	3	21.3	19	5	7	2.90
Williams	3	16.1	12	8	4	6.62
"Clean" White Sox						
Kerr	2	19	14	3	6	1.42
Wilkinson	2	7.1	9	4	3	2.46
James	1	4.2	8	3	2	6.30

NOTE: BB = bases on balls (walks); SO = strikeouts; ERA = earned
run average (runs scored against the pitcher; this is calculated by
dividing the total of earned runs scored against the pitcher by the total
number of innings pitched and multiplying by 9).

Shoeless Joe and the Hall of Fame

In 2000, baseball fans began to lobby for Jackson's inclusion in the Hall of Fame. His impressive career statistics and achievements as a major-league hitter rank him as an equal to some of the sport's greatest sluggers. In August 2001, Shoeless Joe Jackson's famous "Black Betsy" bat was auctioned off in San Jose, California. A collector paid $577,610 for Black Betsy. It is believed to be the highest price ever paid for a baseball bat.[6] It is a tribute to the accomplishments of the bat's original owner. Shoeless Joe has been popularized in movies and plays as one of baseball's most colorful and talented individuals.

Questions for Discussion

1. Do you feel Shoeless Joe Jackson should be allowed to enter Baseball's Hall of Fame? Why?

2. Do you feel the White Sox players should have had separate trials? Explain.

3. Do you think Charles A. Comiskey was partially to blame for the 1919 World Series scandal? Explain.

4. What role did newspapermen play in exposing the 1919 World Series scandal?

5. Do you believe Judge Kenesaw Mountain Landis truly saved the integrity of major-league baseball? Explain your answer.

6. In your opinion, which person deserves the most blame for the 1919 World Series scandal? Is it Chick Gandil? Arnold Rothstein? Or Abe Attell?

7. Was banishment from baseball for life too harsh a penalty for all of the White Sox players? Which players, if any, should not have been banished for life and why?

8. Do you think gambling still affects the outcome of professional and college sporting events?

Chapter Notes

Chapter 1. "Say It Ain't So, Joe"

1. Joe Jackson, "This Is the Truth!" *Shoeless Joe Jackson's Virtual Hall of Fame Page,* n.d., <http://www.blackbetsy.com/jjtruth2.htm> (April 16, 2001).

2. Gene Brown, ed., *The N.Y. Times Encyclopedia of Sports,* vol. 2, Baseball (Danbury, Conn.: Arno Press/Grolier Educational Group, 1979), p. 28.

3. Jackson.

4. Eliot Asinof, *Eight Men Out: The Black Sox and the 1919 World Series* (New York: Holt, Rinehart and Winston, 1963), p. 39.

5. Bruce Lowitt, "Black Sox Scandal: Chicago Throws 1919 World Series," *St. Petersburg Times Online Sports,* December 22, 1999, <www.sptimes/News/122299/sports/Black_Sox_scandal_Ch.shtml> (April 16, 2001).

6. Brown, p. 28.

7. Brad Herzog, *The Sports 100* (New York: MacMillan, 1995), p. 140.

Chapter 2. It's a Money Game

1. David S. Neft, Roland T. Johnson, Richard M. Cohen, *The Sports Encyclopedia: Baseball* (New York: Grosset & Dunlap, 1974), p. 20.

2. Zander Hollander, ed., *The Baseball Book* (New York: Random House, 1982), p. 117.

3. Eliot Asinof, *Eight Men Out: The Black Sox and the 1919 World Series* (New York: Holt, Rinehart and Winston, 1963), p. 21.

4. Ibid., p. 51.

5. "Crisis in Baseball: The Black Sox Scandal of 1919," *About: The Human Internet,* 2001, <wysiwyg://148/http://american history> (April 17, 2001).

6. Gene Brown, ed., *The N.Y. Times Encyclopedia of Sports* (Danbury, Conn.: Arno Press/Grolier Educational Group, 1979), vol. 2, Baseball, p. 23.

7. "The Black Sox Trial: Biographies of Key Figures," *Famous American Trials Page,* n.d., <http://www.law.umkc.edu/faculty/projects/ftrials/blacksox/biographies.html> (June 21, 2001).

8. "Crisis in Baseball: The Black Sox Scandal of 1919."

9. "The History Files: The Black Sox—Charles Comiskey and the White Sox," *Chicago Historical Society Page,* 1999, <http://www.chicagohs.org/History/BlackSox/blk1.html> (June 21, 2001).

10. Bruce Lowitt, "Black Sox Scandal: Chicago Throws 1919 World Series," *St. Petersburg Times Online Sports,* December 22, 1999, <www.sptimes/News/122299/sports/Black_Sox_scandal_Ch.shtml> (April 16, 2001).

11. Victor Luhrs, *The Great Baseball Mystery* (Jamesburg, N.J.: A.S. Barnes & Co., 1966), pp. 40–42.

12. Ibid., p. 86.

13. Asinof, pp. 11–13.

14. Ibid.

15. Luhrs, pp. 106–107.

16. "The Black Sox Trial: The Eight Men Out," *Famous American Trials Page,* n.d., <http://www.law.umkc.edu/faculty/projects/ftrials/blacksox/eightmenout.html> (June 21, 2001).

17. "Crisis in Baseball: The Black Sox Scandal of 1919."

Chapter 3. A Slide Into the Dirt

1. Gene Brown, ed., *The N.Y. Times Encyclopedia of Sports,* vol. 2, Baseball (Danbury, Conn.: Arno Press/Grolier Educational Group, 1979), p. 26.

2. "The Black Sox Trial: The Eight Men Out," *Famous*

American Trials Page, n.d., <http://www.law.umkc.edu/faculty/projects/ftrials/blacksox/eightmenout.html> (June 21, 2001).

3. Joe Jackson, "This Is the Truth!" *Shoeless Joe Jackson's Virtual Hall of Fame Page,* n.d., <http://www.blackbetsy.com/jjtruth2.htm> (April 16, 2001).

4. Brown, p. 26.

5. "The Black Sox Trial: The Eight Men Out."

6. Brown, p. 26.

7. Eliot Asinof, *Eight Men Out: The Black Sox and the 1919 World Series* (New York: Holt, Rinehart and Winston, 1963), p. 57.

8. Jackson.

9. "The History Files: The Black Sox—Gamblers," *Chicago Historical Society Page,* 1999, <http://www.chicagohs.org/history/blacksox/blk2.html> (June 21, 2001).

10. Mac Davis, *Strange and Incredible Sports Happenings* (New York: Grosset & Dunlap, 1975), p. 22.

11. Asinof, pp. 22–23.

12. Victor Luhrs, *The Great Baseball Mystery* (Jamesburg, N.J.: A.S. Barnes & Co., 1966), p. 125.

13. Asinof, p. 26.

14. "The Black Sox Trial: Biographies of Key Figures," *Famous American Trials Page,* n.d., <http://www.law.umkc.edu/faculty/projects/ftrials/blacksox/biographies.html> (June 21, 2001).

15. Brown, p. 26.

16. Ibid.

17. Luhrs, p. 118.

18. Brown, p. 26.

19. "The Black Sox Trial: Biographies of Key Figures."

20. Luhrs, p. 119.

21. Brown, p. 26.

22. Bruce Lowitt, "Black Sox Scandal: Chicago Throws 1919 World Series," *St. Petersburg Times Online Sports,* December 22,

1999, <www.sptimes/News/122299/sports/Black_Sox_scandal_Ch.shtml> (April 16, 2001).

23. Jackson.

Chapter 4. The Scandal That Rocked Baseball

1. Victor Luhrs, *The Great Baseball Mystery* (Jamesburg, N.J.: A.S. Barnes & Co., 1966), p. 42.

2. Gene Brown, ed., *The N.Y. Times Encyclopedia of Sports,* vol. 2, Baseball (Danbury, Conn.: Arno Press/Grolier Educational Group, 1979), p. 26.

3. "Crisis in Baseball: The Black Sox Scandal of 1919," *About: The Human Internet,* 2001, <wysiwyg://148/http://american history> (April 17, 2001).

4. Eliot Asinof, *Eight Men Out: The Black Sox and the 1919 World Series* (New York: Holt, Rinehart and Winston, 1963), p. 96.

5. Ibid., p. 109.

6. "The Black Sox Scandal of 1919."

Chapter 5. Three Strikes, You're Out!

1. David S. Neft, Roland T. Johnson, Richard M. Cohen, *The Sports Encyclopedia: Baseball* (New York: Grosset & Dunlap, 1974), p. 134.

2. Ibid.

3. Eliot Asinof, *Eight Men Out: The Black Sox and the 1919 World Series* (New York: Holt, Rinehart and Winston, 1963), p. 133.

4. Victor Luhrs, *The Great Baseball Mystery* (Jamesburg: N.J.: A.S. Barnes & Co., 1966), p. 112.

5. Ibid., p. 116.

6. Ibid., p. 117.

7. Ibid., p. 119.

8. Ibid., p. 123.

9. Asinof, p. 168.

10. Gene Brown, ed., *The N.Y. Times Encyclopedia of Sports,*

vol. 2, Baseball (Danbury, Conn.: Arno Press/Grolier Educational Group, 1979), p. 26.

11. Ibid.

12. Ibid.

13. Ibid.

14. Ibid.

15. Joe Jackson, "This Is the Truth!" *Shoeless Joe Jackson's Virtual Hall of Fame Page,* n.d., <http://www.blackbetsy.com/jjtruth2.htm> (April 16, 2001).

16. Brown, p. 26.

17. Ibid.

18. David Nemec and Pete Palmer, *1001 Fascinating Baseball Facts* (Lincolnwood, Ill.: Publications International, Ltd., 1994), p. 128.

19. Ibid.

20. Luhrs, p. 185.

21. Asinof, p. 273.

22. Luhrs, p. 195.

Chapter 6. Judgment Day at the Ballpark

1. James Mote, *Everything Baseball* (New York: Prentice Hall Press, 1989), p. 17.

2. "History of the World Series," *The Sporting News Archives,* n.d., <http://www.sportingnews.com/archives/world series/1919.html> (April 16, 2001).

3. "Crisis in Baseball: The Black Sox Scandal of 1919," *About: The Human Internet,* 2001, <wysiwyg://148/http:// american history> (April 17, 2001).

4. Victor Luhrs, *The Great Baseball Mystery* (Jamesburg, N.J.: A.S. Barnes & Co., 1966), p. 206.

5. Ralph Hickock, *A Who's Who of Sports Champions* (Boston: Houghton Mifflin Co., 1995), p. 153.

6. "Shoeless Joe's Bat Sells for $577,610," *The* (Bridgewater, N.J.) *Courier News,* July 22, 2001, p. C-1.

Glossary

acquit—To declare not guilty of a charge.

affidavit—A sworn statement.

attorney—One who acts for a client in a court of law.

bribe—A gift to corrupt the conduct of another; usually money paid in exchange for a favor.

civil action—An action brought to recover some civil right or to obtain redress for some wrong, not a crime or misdemeanor.

confession—An acknowledgement of guilt or wrongdoing.

contract—A written agreement that is legally binding.

convict—To find guilty of an offense, usually by verdict of a judge.

extradition—Delivery of fugitives from justice by one nation or state to another.

grand jury—A jury that decides whether someone should be formally charged with a crime.

indictment—An accusation of a crime or misdemeanor presented in writing by a grand jury.

testimony—Evidence given by a witness under oath.

Further Reading

Asinof, Eliot. *Eight Men Out: The Black Sox and The 1919 World Series.* New York: Henry Holt & Co., 1963.

Frommer, Harvey. *Shoeless Joe and Ragtime Baseball.* Lanham, Md.: Taylor Publishing Co., 1992.

Gropman, Donald. *Say It Ain't So, Joe! The True Story of Shoeless Joe Jackson.* New York: Carol Publishing Group, 1995.

Helmer, Diana Star and Tom Owens. *The History of Baseball.* New York: Rosen, 2000.

Kavanagh, Jack. *Shoeless Joe Jackson.* Broomall, Penn.: Chelsea House Publishers, 1995.

Internet Addresses

The Black Sox Trial
<http://www.law.umkc.edu/faculty/projects/ftrials/
   blacksox/blacksox.html>

History Files—Chicago Black Sox
<http://www.chicagohs.org/history/blacksox.html>

Shoeless Joe Jackson's Virtual Hall of Fame Page
<http://www.blackbetsy.com>

Index

A

Ahearn, Michael, 95, 96
American League, 11, 20, 22, 58
Attell, Abe ("The Little Champ"),
  37–38, 42, 45, 49, 50, 55, 56,
  58, 77, 88, 93, 98, 108
Austrian, Alfred, 82, 86, 89–90,
  95, 106

B

Benton, Rube, 44, 77–78, 110
betting, 22–25
Black Betsy (bat), 103, 116
Black Sox, 6, 9, 80, 92, 94, 99,
  100, 104, 107, 112
Boston Red Sox, 14, 71, 106
Brooklyn Dodgers, 72, 76
Broun, Heywood, 91
Brown, Mr., 45, 46, 78
Brown, Rachael, 88, 93
Burns, "Sleepy" Bill, 35–36, 41,
  42, 44, 45, 49, 55, 58, 62, 78,
  88, 93–94, 96, 98

C

Chandler, Albert B. "Happy," 109
Chapman, Ray, 72
Chase, Charles, 23
Chase, Hal, 24–25, 35, 44, 46, 72,
  78, 88, 93
Chicago Cubs, 12, 73
Chicago Daily News, 6
Chicago Herald and Examiner,
  49
Chicago White Stockings, 11

Cicotte, Eddie, 5, 15, 19, 27, 30,
  34, 36, 38–39, 41, 42, 45–46,
  53, 54, 55, 62, 63, 65, 72, 78,
  80, 81, 82, 84, 88, 92, 97, 98,
  99, 103, 112, 115
Cleveland Indians, 14, 19, 20, 33,
  72, 76, 106
Cobb, Ty, 14, 37, 72, 103, 106
Cohan, George M., 46
Collins, Eddie, 14–16, 33, 52,
  66–67, 114, 115
Collins, Shano, 18, 52, 115
Comiskey, Charles A., 5–6, 8, 11,
  12, 14, 15, 16, 19, 20, 29, 31,
  33–34, 49, 58, 68–70, 72, 73,
  75, 77, 81, 82, 86, 95, 96,
  104, 106, 107, 110, 111
Comiskey Park, 12, 20, 66
Crowe, Robert, 75

D

Daubert, Jake, 22, 53, 54, 57
defense lawyers, 95
Detroit Tigers, 14, 37, 72, 106
Dever, William, 92
Devlin, Jim, 23
Duncan, Pat, 53, 62

E

Eller, Hod, 22, 63, 66
Evans, Nat, 45, 69, 88, 95

F

Faber, Urban "Red," 16
Fallon, William, 38, 93
Felsch, Oscar "Happy," 5, 14, 15,